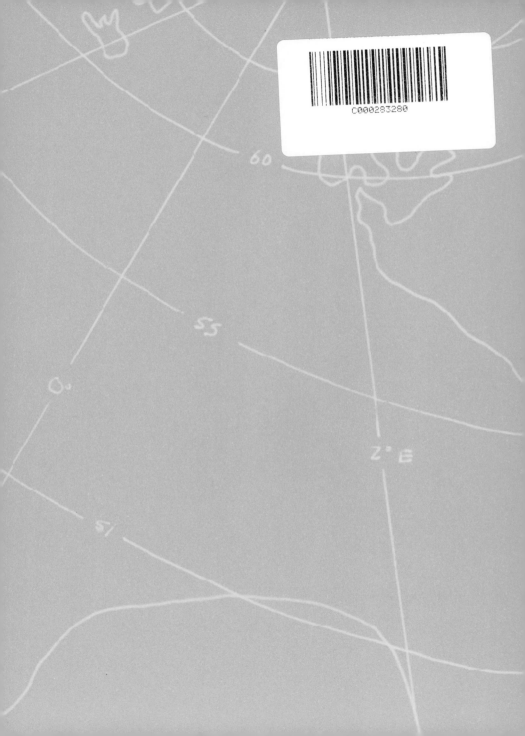

TWO POINTS EAST

Dedicated to the memory of my father,
Jim Ellis

Judith Ellis

TWO POINTS EAST

A View of Maritime Norfolk

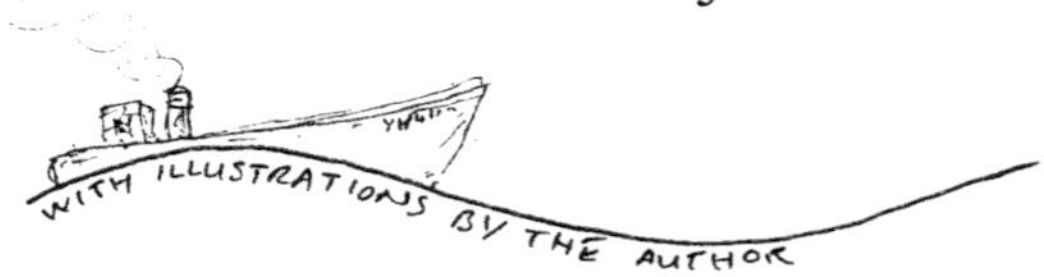

WITH ILLUSTRATIONS BY THE AUTHOR

and a few red herrings

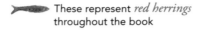 These represent *red herrings*
throughout the book

Published by Judith Ellis
© Judith Ellis 2017

The right of Judith Ellis to be identified
as the author of this work has been asserted
by her in accordance with the Copyright,
Designs and Patents Act, 1988

ISBN 978-1-9997839-0-7

A CIP record for this book
is available from the British Library

Printed and bound in the UK by the Pureprint Group

CONTENTS

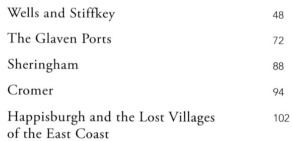

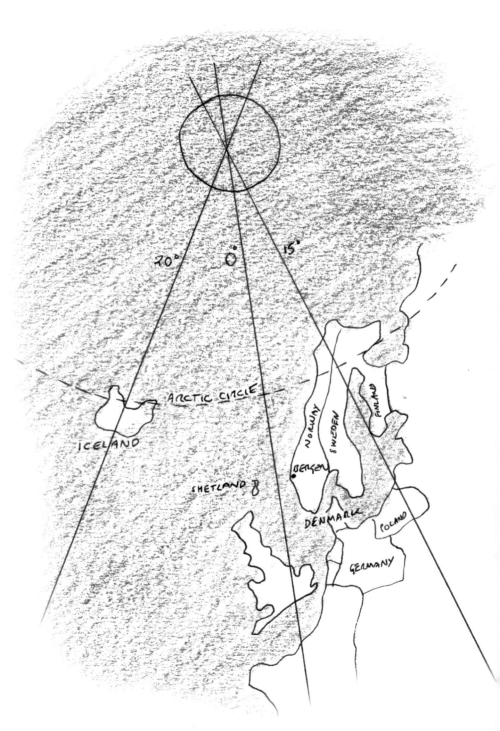

INTRODUCTION

If you stand on the cliffs at Cromer and look northwards, you are facing towards the Arctic. If you were to travel in a straight line just to the east of the Greenwich Meridian, you would pass beyond the North Sea into the Northern Atlantic, leaving Shetland on your left and Bergen in Southern Norway on your right, and you might just catch a glimpse of Iceland at the edge of the Arctic Circle away to your left. To travel with a little more easting would bring you to the Netherlands, Northern Germany and Denmark.

Entering the water between Denmark and Norway, the Skagerrak, would bring you into the Baltic Sea, connecting you with Sweden, Eastern Europe and Russia.

There was a time, not too long ago, when these waters were the workplace for fishermen and sailors from the East Anglian coast, and sea travel was faster and often safer than journeys overland. To these men the sea was not a barrier but a source of food and a means of transport.

This is Britain's youngest coast. The North Sea was formed only 10,000 years ago, when the last ice sheet of the Devensian period melted and the old land of Doggerland gradually flooded, separating East Anglia from mainland Europe.

This eastern edge of Britain is an indeterminate, shifting place, retreating and advancing as sea levels rise and fall, and as storms and surges erode land away here and build up shingle and sand there, forever sculpting the margin between sea and land.

The chalk on which Norfolk rests was laid down 200 million years ago by the slow build-up of tiny marine animals under the sea. In the west of the county the chalk is near the surface, but in the east it lies about 150 feet below. This chalk contains flint, which is the building material of the area.

When the last ice sheet, which came down as far as the north Norfolk coast, began to melt 10,000 years ago, it left deposits of sand, clay and shingle, known as Crag, which make up the features of the landscape here, such as the cliffs from Happisburgh up to West Runton, the Cromer Holt Ridge and the little humps of Beeston Bump and Cley Eye, which visitors always assume are burial mounds.

The area which flooded to become the North Sea, known as Doggerland, was a vast expanse of marsh and sandy soil over which roamed mammoth, deer and wild boar, as well as our Paleolithic ancestors who hunted here and made their tools from flints. Man first came to Norfolk 700,000 years ago, when the ice was here, and left some footprints which were exposed after a storm at Happisburgh and seen for the first time in 2013.

By 2500 BC the Neolithic people had learnt to make bronze, and within another 2,000 years people from Holland and Belgium had arrived with the knowledge of how to smelt iron and the Iron Age was born.

The Romans arrived into this Iron Age community and ruled East Anglia for 400 years. After they had gone, the local people were unable to maintain the infrastructure the Romans had left behind and they reverted to rural life. Angles and Saxons from Northern Germany began to settle here, probably driven away from their own homes by flooding due to rising sea levels.

The Scandinavians followed in the ninth century and the weather began to warm, but between 1200 and 1300 the weather became extreme and there were many floods, famines and storm surges, such as the one which devastated Dunwich in 1286. It was during this period that the peat diggings in Norfolk were flooded, creating the Broads.

The period from 1500 to 1700 was cooler again and has been called a 'Little Ice Age'. Again it brought many storms and bad harvests, but it also coincided with the herring moving their spawning grounds from the Baltic to the North Sea, thereby changing the fortunes of the East Anglian ports for many years.

As we journey round the coast of Norfolk, it becomes apparent how these vagaries of weather affect the rising or falling fortunes of the coastal towns and villages. The devastating three-day storm that permanently blocked up the massive harbour of Dunwich changed the course of the River Blyth. With the river now emerging at Southwold, the small village with no harbour suddenly became the major port along that part of the coast.

Great Yarmouth, which became the world's largest herring fishery, did not exist until the spit of shingle on which it lies built up sufficiently to sustain the building of a town. The process of longshore drift continues to bring sand and shingle down the coast from the north, building up the spits at Yarmouth and Orford, while west of Cromer the same process extends the spits of Blakeney and Scolt Head in a westward direction.

The ports of the north Norfolk coast have been constantly threatened by the silting up of the creeks and rivers, relying on the scouring effect of the tides to keep them navigable. But a port needs a good flowing river to sustain navigation and the relative lack of these, along with the effect of embanking the marshes to gain more land for agriculture, was their final death knell.

This is the story of coastal East Anglia.

KING'S LYNN

King's Lynn marks the beginning of this journey through time and place around the coast of East Anglia. We will take a look at the maritime history of these towns that face the North Sea, through their buildings and their ships, from the smallest of fishing boats to the steam drifters of the early twentieth century; from the medieval sailing cogs of the Hanseatic League to the great sailing tea clippers that boomed briefly before the coming of the steam and then the diesel engine.

Situated on the Wash, facing north towards the North Pole, King's Lynn looks towards Iceland, Scandinavia and the Baltic, rather than France and the Mediterranean. The town of Lynn became Bishop's Lynn when Herbert de Losinga bought the see there. Then, when Henry VIII granted the town a royal charter in 1536, it became King's Lynn.

In the days when it took five days to reach London by road and only two by sea, it was natural for a community of seafarers to look to Northern Europe for trade and adventure.

However, what really distinguished King's Lynn from its neighbouring towns was its connectedness to the hinterland through the Great Ouse

River and its tributaries which linked it by water to Cambridge and the Fens, Bedford and the Midlands.

Walking from the carpark through the busy modern shopping centre towards the river, it is a wonderful surprise to find oneself suddenly in the old part of the town. The streets, one or two blocks away from the river and extending for the best part of a mile north towards the Tuesday Market Place and beyond, are a haven of quiet grandeur. There is very little commercialisation here and the buildings are mostly Georgian or have Georgian façades, with some much earlier ones scattered between.

This is the start of a glimpse into the days when the sea dominated the lives of those who lived and worked on the coast; when storms, or *rages* as they were known, could devastate villages and carry away great chunks of land in one night; when men fished and built ships, mended nets and salted fish; when, indeed, salt was a vital commodity for preserving food in the hard winter months; when the wharves were bustling with Dutch and German sailors, and shipyards were ringing with the sound of the hammers of carpenters and blacksmiths; and the river was swarming with boats of all sizes.

1094

Lynn, not yet King's Lynn, is part of the see of Thetford. Herbert de Losinga, Bishop of Thetford, moves his see to Norwich.

1101

Herbert de Losinga consecrates Norwich Cathedral and two Benedictine monasteries in Yarmouth and Lynn

1145

William de Turbe, the third Bishop of Norwich, builds the Chapel of Ease dedicated to St Nicholas, and endows it with the fees from the Tuesday Market Place built on the Newlands north of the Purfleet River

LYNN'S POSITION ON THE WASH, with its rivers and waterways, gave it access to no fewer than twelve counties as well as London. This is what made it such an important port and so attractive to the merchants of the Hanseatic League.

Early Cog

1204

King John gives Bishop's Lynn a charter granting the merchants some independence from the bishops

1250

All towns of any size were occupied by friars caring for the poor

1271

The Hansa are granted liberties in Lynn but are not allowed to build warehouses

1300

Lynn is thriving as a port exporting wool, cloth, salt, corn and fish, and importing wax, fur, ale and wine

THE HANSEATIC LEAGUE was formed around the middle of the twelfth century by German seafaring merchants. Since there were no navies to protect their cargoes, no international bodies to regulate tariffs and trade, and few ports with regulatory bodies to manage their use, the merchants banded together to establish tariff agreements, provide for common defence and make sure that the ports were maintained.

Wiveton
Cog

The parade of sail, underneath the text, is arranged in order of the development of sailing vessels and their rigs

13

1349

The Black Death leaves just fifty percent of the population surviving

1421

The Trinity Guildhall is rebuilt after being destroyed by a fire

1485

The Battle of Bosworth marks the end of the Wars of the Roses and the beginning of the Tudor Dynasty

TRADE was diminishing as the fifteenth century drew to a close, as it was in many other provincial towns such as York, Hull, Lincoln and Ipswich. This was partly due to the decline of the Hansa merchants but also to the dramatic reduction in population with the Black Death, as well as the general decline in the wool trade.

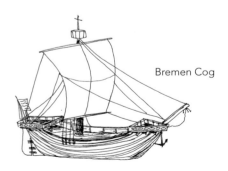

Bremen Cog

1500
Thoresby College is built to house sixteen priests

1534
The Act of Supremacy, making Henry VIII head of the Church of England, begins the weakening of the power of the Church

1536
Henry VIII grants a Royal Charter to claim Lynn from the bishops. It is now named King's Lynn.

THE DISSOLUTION OF THE MONASTERIES in 1536 under Thomas Cromwell meant an end to the lucrative pilgrim traffic to Walsingham and the loss of the monasteries and priory buildings, which were destroyed or sold.

Brig

1547
Death of Henry VIII

1588
The Spanish
Armada

1603
Death of Elizabeth I

King's Lynn is now
exporting more
corn than any other
port in the land,
much of it going to
London by sea

One thousand
collier brigs
bringing coal down
the coast from
Newcastle visited
Lynn in 1603. The
town is now one
of the richest tax
sources in the
realm.

In 1603 the house known as **THE GREENLAND FISHERY**
became an inn. It had been built only two years earlier by
wealthy rope merchant John Atkins, who was forced to sell
it when he lost all his money. For three hundred years it was
used by the whaling fleet. The house still stands and can
be found, looking rather out of place now, right up at the
western end of the quay, opposite a row of flats.

Brigantine

1630
The General
Drainage Act
allows drainage
of the Fens

THE GENERAL DRAINAGE ACT allowed anyone
who could raise the money to drain a fen and claim
ownership of the resulting land, disregarding any commoner's
rights. This enabled existing landowners and other wealthy
men, who came to be known as Adventurers, to enlist the
help of Dutch engineers and start reclaiming land.

CORNELIUS VERMUYDEN built drains, or sokes,
all over the Fens and was knighted for his services.
But his system never really worked properly until
the invention of more efficient pumps, driven by steam
engines rather than wind, for keeping the water out.

Herring Buss

1750
The main trade is
now in coal, corn,
wine and timber.
The port records
show ships arriving
from Danzig, Riga,
Sweden, Denmark,
Leghorn, Oporto
and Lisbon.

CHARLES BURNEY arrives in King's Lynn in 1751
as organist at St Margaret's Church and is courted by
the wealthy as a musician and music teacher. His daughter
FANNY is born the following year. Fanny is to become
famous for publishing a novel, *Emmelina*, in 1778. She
also prepares her diaries for publication and edits her
father's diaries.

Many of the timber BUILDINGS in King's Lynn were
rebuilt or faced with brick during the eighteenth century;
yards with small dwellings also developed, and many new
houses were built. In 1764 the town had eighty-five taverns
and inns. By 1766 one thousand houses had mains piped
water. The Assembly Rooms were also added onto the
Trinity Guildhall in 1766, with a card room and ballroom.

Barque

1792
The Napoleonic
Wars 1792–1815

The cost of living
rose dramatically
during this period,
causing widespread
poverty

With regard to the WHALING INDUSTRY, five whalers
went from King's Lynn each March, returning in July towing
their catch, which was first pumped with air to make each
whale float. The Right Whale floated without the pumped
air, hence its name. On the whalers' return the church bells
would ring and there would be great celebrations. The
blubber was rendered down in a great pit by the river and the
town would be filled with the stench for days.

The WORKHOUSE provided meals for six hundred people
a day, paid for by the Poor Rate – a tax levied on goods.
Hundreds more people received cash payments.

Greenland
Whaler

1847
The coming of the railway
leads to a decline in
coastal trade, but it allows
King's Lynn to undergo
an industrial revolution
servicing agriculture

FREDERICK SAVAGE (1828–1897)

Frederick Savage's company in St Nicholas Street made
iron rakes, cakebreakers for animal feed manufacturers,
steam-powered drills and threshing machines. When
the Alexandria Dock was built, he made cranes and new
machinery. By 1880 he was making fairground roundabouts
and employed 450 men, exporting ploughs and traction
engines to Europe.

ALFRED DODMAN (1832–1908)

Alfred Dodman's Highgate Ironworks, near the Alexandria
Dock, built boilers, pumps and cranes for hospitals,
breweries, ships and mills, which went to locations
as far away as India and South America.

Steam Drifter

THE HANSEATIC LEAGUE: MERCHANTS, MONEY AND POWER IN NORTHERN EUROPE

The Hansa was an alliance, founded in the twelfth century, between the towns of Hamburg and Lübeck, which lay on opposite sides of the Danish Peninsula. It was initially formed to protect the 'Salt Road', the route between the two towns along which salt from the mines at Kiel was traded, but it grew to become an organisation wielding huge power in Northern Europe, controlling the flow of trade and money from the Baltic and North Sea, and from there inland along the rivers connecting deep into Central and Eastern Europe.

By the height of the Hansa's power, merchants from over sixty cities had joined the association. It had no statutes, officials or seals, and all its ships were owned individually. Its families intermarried, thereby ensuring there was always some family member, in whatever place they were trading, to arrange credit or make a deal.

The Hansa economy was based on trust, the merchants' common language of Low German, and family links. The sole business was trade and the pursuit of money, and the sea was their domain over which they exercised unprecedented power. The Hansa policy was protectionist, aimed at producing a German monopoly in the markets the merchants supplied. They raised armies to protect their trade routes and developed their own system of commercial law.

The Hanseatic merchants became wealthy men, commissioning their own portraits and controlling the world of commerce for the best part of three hundred years.

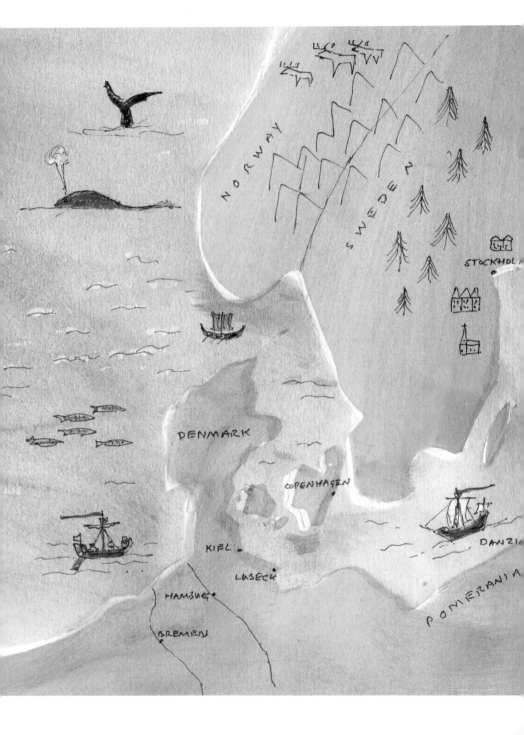

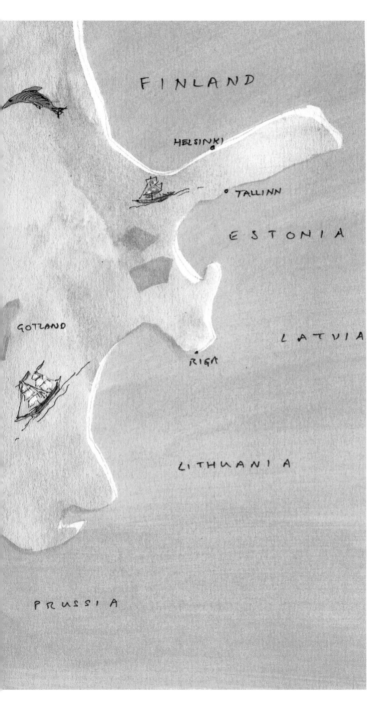

FINLAND

HELSINKI

TALLINN

ESTONIA

GOTLAND

LATVIA

RIGA

LITHUANIA

PRUSSIA

Map showing
Northern Europe
in the 14th century

THE RISE OF LÜBECK

The predominant town in all Hanseatic dealings was Lübeck, which held a central position at the Baltic side of the Danish Sound. Other member cities often complained that the merchants from Lübeck were given advantages over their own merchants.

While most of the cities in the Hansa came within the domains of local feudal lords and their citizens were feudal vassals, Lübeck was one of the few free cities – an imperial city which owed its allegiance to the Emperor alone. This gave Lübeck an advantage over many other cities, added to the fact that it had access to the rich herring fisheries and almost all trade to the Baltic had to go through its port.

The cargoes in the port of Lübeck consisted of salt, herring, grain, honey, amber, ships' stores, and other bulk commodities. It was a steady trade and the Hansa held a monopoly on most of it. This was accomplished not only by the formation of the trade association but also because the Hansa had instigated improvements in the design of the trading vessel of the day – the *cog*.

THE COG

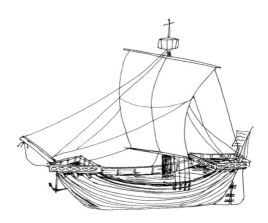

The *cog* first appeared in the tenth century and was widely used, along with the *hulk*, the two probably coexisting for a very long time, but although a number of cogs have been found and excavated, no hulk has yet been discovered, the term only arising from documentary records. The original cogs were the main trading vessels in Northern Europe at this time and they were steered, as were all vessels of the period, not with a rudder but with a steering oar.

But the Limfjord, the main passage between the North Sea and the Baltic, became un-navigable early in the twelfth century due to the problem of its silting up with sand. This meant that the ships had no choice but to sail around the Jutland Peninsula and circumnavigate the dangerous waters off Cape Skagen to get to the Baltic.

Since the ships were steered only with a long oar held by the steersman over the starboard side of the ship (the 'steer board side'), navigation in heavy seas was very difficult, often leading to the loss of a ship. This problem led to the development of the spacious, strong and relatively inexpensive ships needed by the Hanseatic League.

The rig was a single mast with one square sail, and the flat bottom enabled her to sail inland on the rivers. Rigs were built entirely of oak, this being an abundant timber in the Baltic region of Prussia. The timbers were sawn, not split along the grain, which made it much more economical to

above Drawing of the replica of the cog found in Bremen harbour in 1962

25

build, and there was now a rudder mounted on the stern – a revolutionary design which was to spread throughout Europe and the rest of the world. Fore and stern castles were added for protection against pirates, and by the thirteenth century they were decked as well, and the cog was no longer a simple Friesian coaster but had become a sturdy seagoing trader which could cross even the most dangerous of waters.

The first cog to be discovered was found in Bremen harbour in 1962, the year after the *Vasa* was raised from the harbour in Stockholm. A replica of the Bremen cog was built to aid understanding of how it was constructed.

As the Hanseatic League declined towards the end of the sixteenth century, other trade guilds were forming, such as the Merchant Adventurers of England, which traded with the Netherlands and North and West Germany.

A SHORT HISTORY OF THE RUDDER

On the north side of the nave in Winchester Cathedral there stands a font made from a piece of dark limestone brought over from Belgium in 1150 by Henry de Blois, Bishop of Winchester and grandson of William the Conqueror. It is polished so it looks like marble and all around the edge are carvings showing scenes from the life of St Nicholas. On one of its sides there is a carved ship which is the earliest known depiction of a fixed rudder mounted on the stern.

Our understanding of the archaeology of the rudder has been worked out largely by interpretation of carvings like this and models and paintings of early ships. As more early ships are excavated and replicas built to work out both the construction methods and their sailing abilities, so this knowledge is gradually being added to.

The original method of steering any boat was with a steering oar, which we will now refer to as a *quarter rudder*. It can be seen in early depictions of Egyptian boats, Roman triremes and artefacts from ancient China. Its advantage lay in its simplicity and the ease with which it could be replaced should it be damaged or lost at sea. Some quarter rudders were mounted on the stern, but mostly they were side-mounted, with sometimes as many as five in a row if the boat was very large.

A quarter rudder has to be secured to the side of the boat with two fastenings, one a little lower down than the other, but it also needs to be able to rotate about its axis in order to work. A rudder works not by pushing water away from the blade, but more like the wing of an aeroplane, creating lift.

There were various fixing methods used, which usually involved two offset through-beams projecting horizontally through the side of the boat, one below the other. The weight of the rudder was taken on these beams, but lashings were added to prevent it from slipping off. The rudder was operated by a tiller, which was either an upward extension of the shaft or another piece of wood set at right angles to it.

The Greco-Roman rudder was *balanced*, that is, with an equal amount of blade either side of the shaft, but this meant that the shaft protruded from the surface causing turbulence which in turn interfered with efficiency. This problem led to the development of the *unbalanced* rudder, in which the shaft was placed at its leading edge.

Drawing showing the
through-beams and
the fixing of the
quarter rudder

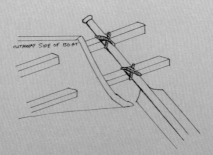

Medieval rudder mounts

The box mount was the commonest of the rudder mounts in medieval times, where two pieces of timber were added across the through-beams, thereby putting less strain on the lashings. The box mount, however, had the big drawback of it being impossible to swing the blade upwards should this foul the bottom or strike something under water.

Damage to rudders was common in those days and of immense importance as ships got bigger. Some quarter rudders were as much as 18 metres long and could weigh up to 11 tons. Spare rudders were usually carried on board.

We are now used to sailing boats with either an additional sail forward of the mast, or with more than one mast. This balanced configuration of sails makes it much easier to turn the boat, as the wind fills the forward sail and helps to blow the bow round, or, conversely, the aftermost sail brings the stern round. But in those days Northern ships had simply one central mast carrying a large square sail and all the steering power had to come from some sort of rudder.

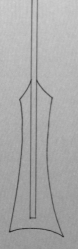

Sometimes the ship was helped to turn by using an extra oar at the front to help push the bow round: this was called a *bow sweep* and this technique was often used on the Viking longships. These narrow, fast vessels had a long keel which enabled the ship to go very fast in a straight line, but they were not so good at turning, much like the Canadian-style touring canoe, as opposed to the almost banana-shaped kayak designed for the rapid turning needed when navigating fast-flowing, rocky waters... Which conjures the thought that maybe the Vikings got as far as the east coast of Canada because it was too difficult to turn round.

A balanced quarter rudder

The development of the rudder in Northern Europe

In the Scandinavian ship-building tradition, which was largely untouched by the Romans, the ships were *double-ended*, that is pointed at both ends, with each plank being overlapped by the one above and internal frames added for strength afterwards.

In time the Viking trading vessel, the *knaar*, eventually developed into the larger *keel*, which became a common merchant vessel in Northern Europe in medieval times.

As the Roman Empire collapsed, the Scandinavian boats began to move southwards, but the system of mounting the quarter rudder remained their weak point. The Viking vessels had a different fixing for the rudder than the Mediterranean ships, relying on a leather thong to secure the upper end, while further down a round oak boss nailed to the side of the boat with a hole in the centre provided the second attachment. A withy or rope was passed through this hole and then through a corresponding hole in the shaft of the rudder.

The withy had to be flexible enough to allow the blade to rotate but strong enough to hold the whole blade securely. But whereas the Mediterranean rudder was supported by structures integral to the boat itself (the through-beams), which absorbed a lot of the stresses placed on the rudder, in the Viking system the withy had to withstand all of the stress and, in addition, the shaft had already been weakened by the hole drilled through it. This system was clearly seriously flawed.

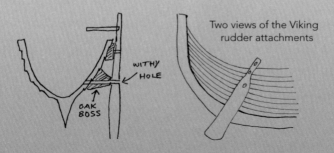

Two views of the Viking rudder attachments

WITHY HOLE

OAK BOSS

By the twelfth century, trade was increasing, and by 1250 the trading vessels of the time, the cog and the hulk, had five times the capacity of the eleventh-century knaar, and loss of the rudder was becoming a problem.

Why didn't the Northern shipwrights know about the stronger Mediterranean fixings?

At first it would seem strange that the ship-builders of Western Europe would not have known about the Mediterranean ships, as you would think that their ships would have been frequent visitors to the southern ports. But in fact the strong surface currents in the Mediterranean running from west to east through the Straits of Gibraltar made it easy to sail *into* the Mediterranean but very difficult to sail out again with the relatively primitive sailing rigs of the time, added to which was the hazard of running the gauntlet of the hostile Muslim ships of Spain and North Africa guarding the waters.

This meant that most of the trade with the Mediterranean had to be carried out overland and, although a traveller would have seen the local ships, they would not have been able to describe the technicalities of the fixings accurately enough for a shipwright to emulate them. Just when the need for innovation was most strong, the northern ship-builders remained technologically isolated.

Step up the gudgeon and pintle

The gudgeon and pintle form a hinge, which blacksmiths had been making for a long time, for the hanging of gates. The genius idea of the shipwrights, however, was to use this hinge for attaching the rudder to the sternpost of a ship, thereby giving it support all the way down its length.

The *pintle* is a metal spike attached to the rudder by a metal strap, and the *gudgeon* is a corresponding metal strap on the stern of the ship carrying a hole into which the pintle can drop. Not only did the gudgeon and pintle solve the problem of attaching a rudder securely to a ship, but it also led to a major change in the design of the hull, and subsequently enabled the development of the three-masted, fully rigged ship of the mid-fourteenth century.

The reason for this lay in the fact that most early ships had curved sterns. Attaching the new rudder to a curved sternpost made it difficult to remove at sea should it become damaged. The proximity of the curved hull to the leading edge of the rudder also made for a lot of turbulent water surrounding the rudder blade, which interfered with its efficiency.

Step up the vertical sternpost

As you can see in the drawing at bottom right, using a vertical sternpost not only made removal of the rudder much easier, but it also introduced a gap between the hull and the rudder which had to be filled in with wood. This wood, known as *deadwood*, effectively made a fin. The fin not

only reduced the turbulence but added to the turning power of the rudder and, by acting a bit like the feathers on an arrow, it also gave the ship extra stability.

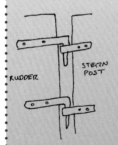

RUDDER

STERN POST

By the mid-fourteenth century an extra mast had been added to most big ships, allowing for the wind to aid the turning of the stern. This paved the way for the three-masted, fully rigged ship, which, with the gudgeon and pintle rudder and vertical sternpost, allowed much larger ships to be built that could be handled with a great deal more ease and safety. This innovation was gradually adopted by ships from Europe and was to spread worldwide.

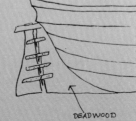

DEADWOOD

With the use of an ordinary metal hinge, the North Sea ship-builders had begun the subsequent rapid developments of ship design. It is one of the milestones of maritime history, and the gudgeon and pintle remains the standard fitting for rudders to this day.

'A Well-Cut Oar'

In *The Odyssey*'s 'The Book of the Dead', the goddess Circe provides a favourable wind to bring Odysseus to the 'deep flowing River of Ocean and the frontiers of the world, where the fog-bound Cimmerians live in the City of Perpetual Mist'.

Here, with his sharp sword, Odysseus digs a trench a cubit long and a cubit wide into which he pours libations to the dead, of honey and milk, sweet wine and barley. Hoping to speak with the prophet Tiresias, he offers, on his return to Ithaca, to make Tiresias a sacrifice of his finest black sheep. Then cutting the throat of a convenient sheep, he pours the dark blood into the hole he has just dug and the Souls of the Dead begin to appear.

After a heartbreaking encounter with Elpenor, one of Odysseus's shipmates who had died earlier, the blind seer Tiresias appears with a gold rod in his hand, drinks the dark blood and begins to prophesy. He predicts that, after many troubles on his way home to Ithaca, Odysseus will find his wife Penelope beset by suitors who are living in his house, eating his food and pressing Penelope with offers of wedding gifts. When Odysseus has cleared his palace of the suitors Tiresias instructs him to:

> 'take a well-cut oar and go on until you reach a people who know nothing of the sea and never use salt with their food, so that our crimson-painted ships and long oars that serve those ships as wings are quite beyond their ken. And this will be your cue – a very clear one, which you cannot miss. When you fall in with some other traveller who speaks of the "winnowing fan" you are carrying on your shoulder, the time has come for you

to plant your shapely oar in the earth and offer Lord Poseidon the rich sacrifice of a ram, a bull and a breeding-boar. Then go back home and make ceremonial offerings to the immortal gods who live in the broad heavens, to all of them this time, in due precedence. As for your own end, Death will come to you in his gentlest guise. When he takes you, you will be worn out after an easy old age and surrounded by prosperous people. This is the Truth that I have told you.'

It seems strange that Odysseus should take only one oar with him – anyone who has rowed a boat will know that with just one oar your boat will go round in circles – but perhaps if the 'well-cut oar' was a steering oar, the metaphor begins to take on a deeper meaning.

KONTORS AND STEELYARDS

The *kontor*, also referred to as a *steelyard* or *stalhof*, was the overseas headquarters of the Hansa. The four main ones were located in Novgorod, Bergen, Bruges and London.

The *kontor* in London was a walled, quayside settlement where as many as four hundred people lived. It was a bit of Germany within England. As what we call Germany now was many small states then, the *kontor* was the nearest thing to a connected idea of Germany.

The young men of the Hansa families were sent off to sea to learn their trade, and the *kontor* in Bergen held brutal 'games' each year for the apprentice merchants who had to undergo keel hauling, beatings and other hardships to prove their worth. Dedicated to their world of trade and money, the Hansa could be ruthless operators.

Under the normal code for sailors, the captain of a ship had the prerogative to decide if it was safe to put to sea and to jettison the cargo, should it be deemed necessary for the safety of the ship. The Hansa vessels answered only to the merchant and the captain could have his ears cut off for refusing to obey.

> *The steelyard in London was where Cannon Street station is now. It is marked with a plaque on the wall just below the bridge and with the naming of the adjacent Steelyard Passage. The plaque was placed there in 2005 to celebrate Anglo-German relations and can be seen if you look up at the bridge from the Thames Footpath.*

HANSEATIC CONNECTIONS WITH THE WASH

Boston and Lynn attracted the German merchants for their wool and their annual summer markets, Lynn particularly for its connections through the river to its hinterlands. Both of these towns had warehouses belonging to the Hansa but they were not *kontors*, and the Hansa merchants were not granted the right to own their houses, they had to lodge with the local *burgesses* instead.

Boston had a particular connection with Lübeck, and Lynn with Danzig and Bremen; Hull with Prussia, Great Yarmouth with Hamburg, and Cologne with Ipswich.

There was a transfer of artisans and sailors between the Wash and the Baltic seaports, and records show a community of German shoemakers working in Lynn in 1420.

When in 1449 English privateers seized the ships of the salt fleet which was sailing from southwest France to the Baltic, a deterioration began in England's commercial relationships with the Hansa, until, after another incident with Denmark, this time in 1468, all of the Hanseatic towns finally broke off their relations with England.

Peace was eventually negotiated at the Treaty of Utrecht in 1474, when the Germans insisted on the free gift of their trading posts in Boston and London and a new one to be built in Lynn. The new warehouse was built in 1475 between the river and the Saturday Market Place. In 1751 it was bought by Edward Everard and part of its east wing was incorporated into the new house he had built. Known as St Margaret's House it can still be seen opposite St Margaret's Church.

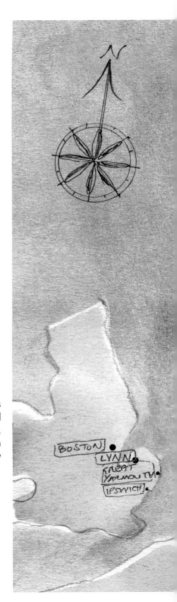

Map showing the positions of the major towns and cities trading with Lynn, Boston and Ipswich during the 15th century

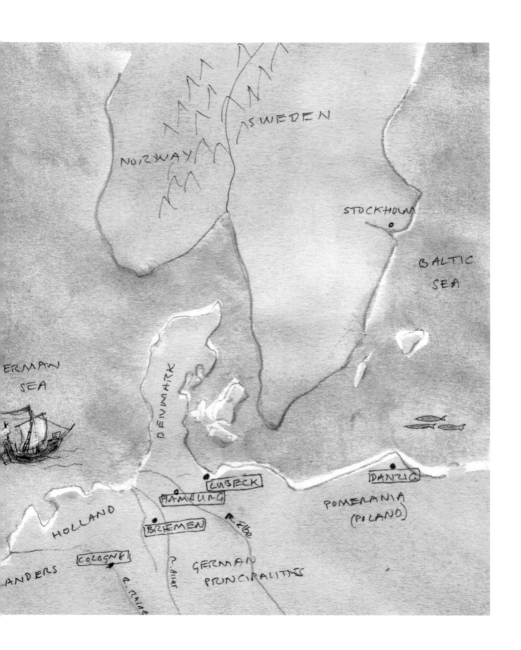

NORWAY

SWEDEN

STOCKHOLM

BALTIC
SEA

GERMAN
SEA

DENMARK

ERMAN
SEA

LUBECK

HAMBURG

DANZIG

HOLLAND

BREMEN

R. Oder

POMERANIA
(POLAND)

COLOGNE

ANDERS

R. Alier

GERMAN
PRINCIPALITIES

R. Rhine

37

THE TUESDAY MARKET PLACE was laid out by William de Turbe, the third bishop of Norwich, as Lynn had by now become a flourishing town. It was built on the Newlands in the twelfth century, almost doubling the size of the town.

Markets were vital places for ordinary people to be able to buy and sell food and other essential items. There were taxes levied on the markets, and in this case, the bishop endowed his new Chapel of Ease with its income.

The Shrine of Our Lady at Walsingham is one of Britain's earliest shrines and marks where a vision of the Virgin Mary appeared in 1061

ST NICHOLAS STREET
LEADING TO ST.NICHOLAS
CHAPEL

ST NICHOLAS CHAPEL was built in 1145 as a Chapel of Ease for the many pilgrims passing through on their way to Walsingham. It was rebuilt in 1200.

A chapel does not have a font and cannot be used to baptise or marry people. This kept the fees for baptism and marriage firmly in the hands of the Benedictine monks.

The font in Morston Church has graffiti marks of pilgrims' feet scratched around its base

By the beginning of the seventeenth century, King's Lynn was comparable commercially to Bristol, exporting more corn than any other port in the realm, with most of it going to London.

Its waterways connected it with twelve counties, and trade links were well established with Norway, Greenland, Iceland, the Baltic and the Low Countries.

Coal came down the coast from Newcastle and then was taken inland from King's Lynn. The port records show that, in 1608 alone, one thousand colliers came to King's Lynn and among the goods that were sent back were corn, butter, cheese, hides and wool.

Many of the town's important buildings were erected or embellished during the seventeenth century.

THE DUKES HEAD HOTEL was built in 1684 to accommodate the increasing numbers of merchants visiting the town.

It was commissioned by wealthy rope-maker and Member of Parliament for King's Lynn, John Turner, who the year before had built the Merchant Exchange, later to become the Custom House. The architect for both of these buildings was Henry Bell. The duke commemorated in the name of the hotel was the Duke of York, brother to the King.

BRICKMAKING

During the seventeenth century with increasing mercantile wealth, many of the earlier timber buildings were either replaced or faced with brick or stone from the friaries which had fallen into disuse after the dissolution of the monasteries in 1536. Fires were a constant hazard for timber buildings, and the increasing wealth of the town allowed for the use of more expensive materials.

Brick clay was dug locally and pressed into brick moulds before drying and firing. The bricks were *skintled*, stacked for drying, on edge, a fraction apart. If adjacent bricks were touching, a mark would be left on the bricks and these marks are known as *skintlings*. The earlier bricks were stacked diagonally and the later ones horizontally, leading to either diagonal or horizontal marks. If you look carefully, you can often find *skintling* marks on some of the bricks of old buildings.

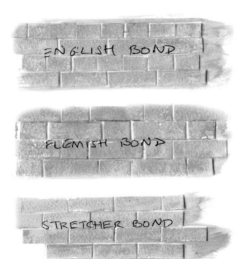

Walls were built two bricks deep for strength and linked by alternating the orientation of adjacent bricks, leading to a pattern called the bond. *English bond*, alternate rows of headers and stretchers, was soon superseded by *Flemish bond*. The sketch on the left shows a detail of three walls demonstrating three different types of bonds. The top one is English bond, the middle one is Flemish bond, and the bottom one

opposite The Custom House, built by Henry Bell in 1863, stands on the waterfront and is now the Tourist Office

right This fine bronze statue of George Vancouver stands by the river in front of the Custom House

stretcher bond. The bricks in stretcher bond are simply for facing an existing wall, as there are no bricks end-on which can bond it with a second layer of bricks behind.

GEORGE VANCOUVER (1755–1795)

George Vancouver was born in King's Lynn, the son of the assistant collector of taxes at the port. His father's links to the maritime world secured him a position on the *Resolution* under James Cook. It was under Cook that

Vancouver learned his craft of seamanship, navigation and surveying, making such an impression that he was asked to join Cook's third voyage to the Pacific in 1776.

On his return from the Pacific, Vancouver was commissioned as lieutenant in the Royal Navy and had a number of years sailing in the West Indies before being asked to undertake an expedition to the west coast of America. His mission was to make a detailed survey of the entire coastline, to settle a matter with the Spanish commissioner of damage claims over an incident in Nootka, and to establish whether an entry to a possible Northwest Passage existed. Vancouver's ships, the *Discovery* and *Chatham*, left Falmouth on 21st April 1791, and this lengthy voyage established him as one of the great chart-makers.

He struck up an unexpected friendship with the Spanish commissioner, whose name was Juan Francisco de la Bodega y Quadra. The commissioner asked his new friend to name an island after both of them, and so Vancouver gave the place where they met the name of Quadra and Vancouver's Island. It is now abbreviated to just Vancouver Island.

On his return in 1795, Vancouver retired to Petersham, where he had almost completed writing the account of his journeys before he died, aged only forty.

SEAHENGE

In the spring of 1998, a low tide revealed an oak post in the sands at Holme beach. A local person with an interest in archaeology monitored the site and informed the Norfolk Museum Service. As the summer wore on, more posts were revealed by the eroding sands and a circle of roughly 21 metres was exposed. English Heritage and the Norfolk Archaeological Unit excavated the site the following year.

Named Holme1, but christened 'Seahenge' by the local media, it comprised of a circle of closely packed oak posts all originally about 3 metres in

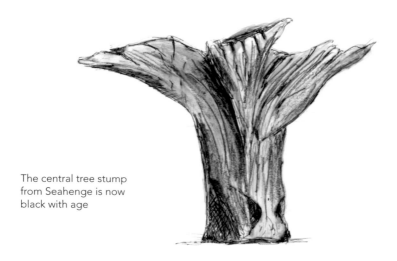

The central tree stump from Seahenge is now black with age

length, surrounding a great upturned tree stump. With the use of dendro-chronology, it has been established that the trees were probably felled in 2049 BC.

That far back in time, the area would have been saltmarsh separated from the sea by dunes and mudflats. But with the progressive change from saltmarsh to freshwater reed swamp, and then to alder carr, a process that has been echoed for centuries all around this coast, the natural decay of vegetation gradually led to the formation of peat. It was this peat that made the ideal conditions for the preservation of the timber. The gradual encroachment of the sea and the shifting of the sands eventually led it to emerge, in its current position, from the sands on Holme beach.

Archaeologists, with their flair for informed creative thinking, are of the opinion that it was used for a burial rite, with the body being laid on the tree stump to be picked clean by scavenging birds – a ritual known as *excarnation*. No human remains have been found at the stump, however, only some honeysuckle rope which was used to drag it into place.

Drawing made from a photograph of Seahenge before its removal

Another timber circle was subsequently discovered 100 metres further east. Named Holme2 it was decided not to excavate it, possibly because of the local protest over Holme1 when many local people wanted it left undisturbed.

The timbers of the first circle were removed and taken to the Fenland Archaeological Trust Field Centre at Peterborough where, after initial cleaning, they were put into tanks of fresh water to begin the process of desalination. Ancient wood deteriorates very quickly on exposure to air, and the next stage was to soak the timber in a tank of wax-emulsified water. These techniques of wood conservation have been pioneered by conservators involved in the preservation of old ships, notably the *Vasa* in Stockholm, and have also been used on the *Mary Rose* in Portsmouth.

Wood deteriorates when its cellular structure starts to break down and water leaches out of the cells. The aim of the treatment is to replace the water with Poly Ethylene Glycol, PEG, a wax-like chemical which supports the internal structure of the cell and prevents its collapse. This process takes several years. The final stage is to vacuum-freeze-dry the wood to remove any remaining water.

'Seahenge' is now in the King's Lynn Museum.

The correct description of the circle is a mortuary enclosure. The word 'henge' usually means a structure with a ring bank and ditch, sometimes with stone structures as well.

WELLS AND STIFFKEY

First known as Guella, the Saxon word for a spring, Wells has no river connecting it to inland towns, and so could never achieve the same importance as the great ports of King's Lynn and Great Yarmouth. Harbours on the shallow waters of Norfolk's east coast also need a river to help to scour out the sand and silt which comes in on every tide. Despite these disadvantages, Wells thrived for several hundred years as a base both for fishing and ship-building.

The first recorded evidence for a harbour in Wells is a reference to Hereward the Wake, who is recorded as taking ship from here to escape the siege on his hold-out in Ely in 1070. It is thought by some that the first harbour used to be alongside the church and, although there does not seem to be any documentary evidence for this, there is a street named Staithe Place near the church (*staithe* being an old word for landing place). The land was owned by Ramsey Abbey and was given a charter by King John granting the rights of a trading port for corn, salt and reeds for thatching. The town supplied Flanders and occasionally London with grain, and was granted a market in 1202.

There is no record in Domesday of any sea fishing being done in Wells at this time, only river fishing which was mostly done by setting traps for perch, bream, tench, pike, salmon and eels. But by the twelfth century commercial fisheries were starting to develop, with fishermen venturing as far as the Norwegian coast to catch herring. The Hanseatic League soon put a stop to this, protecting their monopoly by prohibiting the fishermen from salting Norwegian herring. Turning to cod instead, by 1357 they were fishing regularly in Icelandic waters, paying tax on the cod to the Norwegians at the staple port of Bergen.

Fish was an important part of the medieval diet, partly due to the requirement for so many fasting days during the Church's calendar, on which no meat was to be eaten. Fridays were fast days, as were the forty days of Lent, and other days were added to this, making at one point a total of one hundred and forty days in one year. This changed after the accession of Elizabeth I, when fasting was no longer necessary. The resulting decreased demand for fish led to a fall in prices until it was realised that with fewer fishermen there would be fewer seamen available to serve in the Navy. The Friday fast was reinstated, but the increase in piracy with large, armed privateers operating out of Dunkirk made life very difficult. The final nail in the coffin for the fishing trade was the Salt Tax introduced by Charles I, a tax he was able to levy without approval from Parliament. With the increase in the cost of salting the fish, the fishery never really recovered.

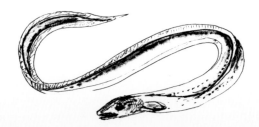

THE SECRET LIFE OF THE EEL

To the east of Florida, a little beyond the Bermuda Triangle and just inside the great mid-Atlantic Ridge, lies the Sargasso Sea. Deep blue in colour, with exceptionally clear water, where visibility is up to 200 metres, it earned its name from the rafts of Sargassum seaweed which are swept into it by the surrounding currents.

The Gulf Stream to the west, the Canary current to the east and the Atlantic currents to the north and south create a vortex of water which the early Portuguese navigators called the *volta do mar* and which we now call the North Atlantic Gyre. This is the setting for that most mysterious of aquatic fish – the eel.

For centuries eels were a staple food source for communities living by the sea, but where they bred was not discovered until a Danish marine biologist, Johann Schmidt, began his research in 1902. The tiny larvae of the eel, the *leptocephali*, had already been found in the Atlantic, and Schmidt began by trawling samples from different areas of the ocean, gradually tracking down the location of their greatest concentration to the Sargasso Sea.

There he found them in large numbers, but to his surprise, he noticed that the *leptocephali* of the European Eel were mixed in equally large concentrations with those of the American Eel. After twenty years of dedicated and persistent research, interrupted by the War, Schmidt was able to unravel part of the mysterious life cycle of the eel.

As the tiny *leptocephali* feed and grow, they become *glass eels*, so called because of their lack of pigment. Looking like tiny transparent ribbons with a pair of black eyes at one end, the European glass eels swim eastwards to the coasts of Europe while the American ones turn west to the coast of America. It is thought that before the tectonic plates under the ocean shifted to form the mid-Atlantic Ridge they were all one species, and only since then have they evolved into two separate species.

When the glass eels reach our coast they swim up into the rivers, developing pigmentation as they go, becoming *elvers*, still only a few inches long. No-one yet understands the trigger for the glass eel to alter its metabolism to be able to live in fresh water.

As it grows, the glass eel develops a brownish-yellow colour and becomes a *yellow eel*. It takes 15 years for an eel to mature into a breeding adult, by which time it has changed colour yet again, this time into a gunmetal blue, and is now called a *silver eel*.

Something now triggers the silver eel to begin its journey back to the spawning ground. It will make its way down to the estuary, crossing where necessary over marshland and wet sand to get there. On arrival it spends much time feeding in preparation for the long journey to the Sargasso Sea and will put on 28% of its weight in body fat.

It undergoes a strange metamorphosis now. The eyes enlarge and the retina turns blue for better vision in the depths of the ocean where there is very little light. The body adapts to a saltwater environment again and develops the ability to withstand the enormous pressure of the deep ocean. Finally the digestive system atrophies, as the eel will never feed again.

Adult eels have never been seen to reproduce. No adults have ever been found in the Sargasso Sea and the migration across the Atlantic has never been observed. More recent work involved tagging some adults and tracking their migration, but after six months only seven of the twenty marked eels were found and they were only a third of the

way across the ocean. Could it take over a year to reach the breeding grounds? How do they survive for that long without feeding? Are they living at such depths that they cannot be tracked?

What we do know is that the numbers of the American and European Eel are declining, and with so little understanding of their life cycle and the changing environment their survival is now under question.

THE WELLS FISHERY

Wells currently has a small but thriving commercial fishery supplying lobsters and crabs to the catering industry. The fishermen come from families with a long tradition of fishing, and some of their stories have been recorded and can be heard at Rescue Wooden Boats based at Stiffkey.

Lobster pots are now made from a durable form of plastic, but there are still some makers of traditional willow pots

WELLS HARBOUR ACT

In 1663 an Act was passed for the improvement of the harbour, authorising the imposition of levies on every cargo going in and out of the port. Two collectors were employed to collect the dues, and the money raised was to be used for the maintenance of the buoys, beacons, channels and harbour.

Wells bait sheds

EMBANKMENTS

The development of agriculture in the eighteenth century, with the need to produce more food for an increasingly urbanised population, led to clashes between the landowners, who wanted to drain the marshes to reclaim more land, and the fishermen and merchants, who needed the waterways maintained for shipping.

An embankment prevented the tide bringing the sea in over the enclosed marsh, and over a period of about thirty years or so the rain would gradually wash the salt out of the soil. This created better pasture for sheep and cattle, which were traditionally grazed on the saltmarsh. Some of the old drove roads can still be seen as tracks leading down to the marsh from the coast road.

The local landowners were the Cokes of Holkham and the Turners from Wells, and between them they were responsible for three banks which are still

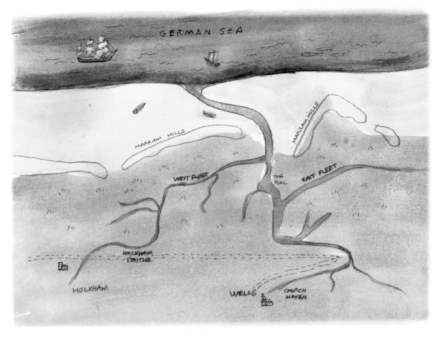

Wells before the embankments were built

in existence. In 1719 the Cokes built a bank west of the harbour, which can still be seen today, stretching out towards Holkham through the salt marshes west of Beach Road. Two years later, Charles Turner, a landowner from Wells who was also the Member of Parliament for Wells, built a bank to the east of the harbour: this is where the present sea wall with its footpath leads east towards Stiffkey. His son, John Turner, then built a third bank, extending the existing one, in 1758.

But the perennial problem with so many of these marshy coastlands has always been the silting up of the waterways, resulting in restriction to navigation. The best harbours were served by rivers, which provided channels through which the sand and silt brought in by the tide could be flushed back

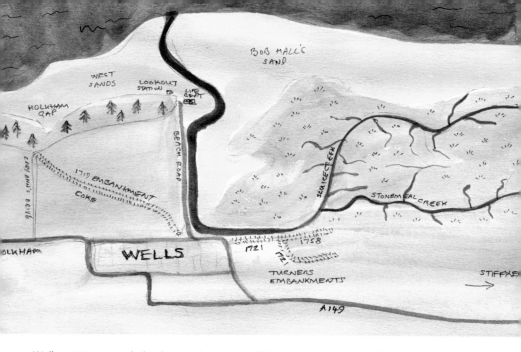

Wells as it is now, with the three embankments. This map shows how the channel from the harbour out to sea has been straightened, with Beach Road running alongside it. The Marram Hills were planted by the Cokes with Scots Pine between 1865 and 1895 to consolidate the dunes. These were later replaced by a species of pine more tolerant of maritime conditions.

on the ebb by the outgoing river. King's Lynn was well served by the Great Ouse, but Wells was not so well situated and the new embankments interfered with this natural system.

The conflict between the landowners and the merchants and fishermen eventually led to a court case. This case went to court three times before John Turner's bank was ordered to be removed, by which time Turner had died. But only thirty-five years later, Coke was given permission to rebuild the bank, as long as he also built a tidal reservoir from which water could be released every few days to flush out the silt brought in by the tide. He got his bank, but he never built the reservoir. The Cokes went on to build another embankment east of Burnham in the 1660s.

MALTING

Malt was produced commercially in Wells from the sixteenth century, and by 1800 there were eleven maltings in the town between Glebe and Standard Roads. During the eighteenth century the demand for malt increased, as London was growing in size and needed more malt for brewing. Maltings take up a lot of space, and need the circulation of clean air and a ready supply of grain, which placed Wells with its harbour in a good position to both produce and export malt by sea to London to meet this increasing market.

The Dutch used malt for making gin and Holland was a good market for the Wells maltsters, but when the French sided with America in the American War of Independence, it made the passage of ships from Holland to East Anglia too hazardous and Holland had to source its malt in the Baltic instead.

The Maltings building still standing in the town was built in the early nineteenth century, but by the Depression in the 1920s demand had declined and the owners, F & G Smith, closed down their malting business. The building has four floors at the south end and two at the north end where the kiln was located. The capacity of the *steep*, where the grain was soaked, was 48 *quarters*, a quarter being a volume of grain weighing 1/20th of a ton.

Barley has been malted worldwide for centuries to make beer and for use in various foods, and there is archaeological evidence that settlers as early as Neolithic times in Britain and Switzerland were malting barley, wheat and rye. Today it is still used for making beer, whisky, malt-flavoured drinks and cereals, and various baked foods, including rich tea biscuits.

The light soils of East Anglia are ideal for the cultivation of malting barley, which continues to this day.

HOW IS MALT MADE?

Drying

The grain is first spread out on the malting floor in a layer about 4 inches deep where it is allowed to dry until the moisture content is below 14%. It is

The Old Granary on the quay is now converted into apartments

then stored for six weeks to overcome the problem of seed dormancy which would inhibit the start of germination.

Steeping

The grain is then soaked in water in a large drainable tank called a steep. This is usually located on the ground floor of the maltings and the grains are drained and rinsed over three days, by which time they should have a moisture content of about 46%.

Couching

The soaked grain is then transferred to the germinating, or couching, floor where the sprouting grains are constantly turned around as they dry. The temperature is gradually raised and the moisture controlled by sprinkling with water. As the grain germinates, the starches are slowly converted into sugar, and at this stage it is called *green malt*.

Kilning

When all the starches have been converted to sugar, germination is stopped by drying in a kiln. The green malt is laid on a floor made of wire mesh, perforated tiles or wooden slats, above the kiln, for three days.

The temperature is raised to about 55°C by channelling smoke from the *oasting* fireplace through the grain until it reaches the desired colour, which may be very pale or continued through amber to chocolate or black malt.

The malt was then sold to be made into beer by the breweries, but often the farm which had grown the barley would see the whole process through from the growing of the grain to the making of the beer. Before the rise of commercial breweries it was common for inns and big houses to malt and brew their own beer.

To produce beer, the malt is ground up and boiled with water to extract the sugars, and then fermented with hops and yeast. The hops both flavour and preserve the beer. Without the hops the beer would not last very long.

SHIP-BUILDING

There were two shipyards in Wells, which, along with those in King's Lynn, were the main centres for ship-building on the north Norfolk coast. The two yards were sited next to each other on the east end of the quay, near Jolly Sailor Yard, and the ships were built outside on the shore.

Each shipyard needed a slipway and access to deep water, a forge, and a floor on which the frames could be marked out to full size. There was no dry dock, but there was instead a heavy timber gridiron on the shore onto which a ship could be grounded at low tide for repairs to be carried out.

Local oak and elm was used, but a lot of pine, for planking and spars, was imported from Scandinavia and North America.

🐟 *It was fashionable then to paint a ship with false gun ports along her sides*

The gantry of the old granary building, such a striking feature of the waterfront, is now part of the conversion of the entire building into flats

The planks were sawn in a pit, with the skilled sawyer on top guiding the saw. Sawyers were often itinerant and had a reputation for drinking a great deal of beer.

A shipwright and a ship's carpenter were apprenticed, often from the age of 12 or 13, for seven years, and the 1841 census records Wells as having eleven shipwrights.

A forge was a necessity for making all the metal fittings such as bolts, nails and the chainplates which are the metal straps on the hull for the attachment of the rigging holding the masts in place.

A blacksmith, who was also apprenticed for seven years, worked only in iron, whereas the whitesmith, or tinsmith, worked the lighter metals such as tin, brass and copper, and they were able to make fittings such as navigation lamps.

If a ship was to be used in the tropics, her bottom was sheathed in copper for protection against burrowing molluscs such as the Toredo Worm.

Anchors, cables, chains and winches were generally bought in, and Wells had a sailmaker, a blockmaker (a block on a ship is a wooden pulley) and a rope-maker – all essential trades for a ship-building town.

Henry Tyrell was, perhaps, the most well-known shipwright, and he built many fine ships including the brig *The Countess of Leicester* in 1847. She was built for the southern trade, taking cured herring to the Mediterranean and bringing back oranges and dried fruit.

PIERHEAD PAINTINGS

During the eighteenth century many ships' captains owned their own ships, often collectively with the ship's builder and sometimes with members of the crew as well. Taking a great pride in their vessels, they would commission paintings to be done of their ships, and a new breed of ship artists appeared.

above A pierhead painting of a Lowestoft smack by John Gregory in the author's possession. Oil on board.
opposite A pierhead painting of *The Countess of Leicester*

These men were often sign-writers and sometimes retired seamen with a gift for painting. Their work, always naive in style, usually portrays a side-on view of a ship under full sail. Lacking the finesse of a trained artist, their paintings have a lively quality and bring an accuracy of detail with every block and reefing point closely observed, revealing the artist's intimate knowledge of his subject.

When a ship came into port, the painters would approach the captain for a commission to paint his ship, and these men became known as *pier-head painters*.

Sometimes oil on board or canvas, sometimes watercolour or gouache, and sometimes even painted on glass, these paintings would take pride of place above many a seaman's mantelpiece. The painter's reference point for art was often the local inn-sign or crude picture books, but what was valued above all else was accuracy of detail and the authenticity of the ship portrayed.

Pierhead paintings are now becoming sought after and, although not always signed, certain characteristics of individual painters can be recognised.

The work of various East Anglian pierhead painters from the turn of the nineteenth century can still be found. Thompson Swann was a Yarmouth fisherman who retired to a life of painting and innkeeping, selling his work over the bar in the Old Commodore Tavern in Gorleston; P. Gregory was

a Lowestoft sign-writer working in oils; and John Gregory (1840–1917) worked from both Lowestoft and Yarmouth. Works of Lowestoft smacks and trawlers by E. G. Tench and J. T. Boyne can also still be found.

THE SHARPIE

The sharpie was a long, narrow, shallow-drafted racing dinghy designed in 1931 in Bremen, where the first medieval cog was found. It was designed to be easy for home building, with its flat-sided plywood construction, and was the nominated dinghy for the 1956 Olympic Games in Australia, being superseded at the following Games by the Flying Dutchman. The gaff-rigged sail was originally 12 square metres but is now 16, making for fast, exciting sailing. There are about sixty remaining sharpies in Britain.

Wells harbour from the east side where the shipyards were sited, building ships on the shore. Wells Sailing Club operates from the east end of the harbour and sails some of the few remaining sharpies.

FRANK DYE (1928–2010)

Frank Dye is renowned in the world of small-boat sailing for his two crossings of the North Sea in a 15 foot 10 Wayfarer sailing dinghy. The first of these expeditions, in 1963, was to Iceland, and the second to Norway the following year. Each passage covered a distance of 650 miles.

Dye and his crew survived capsizing four times on the Norway voyage, force 8 and 9 gales, and broken rigging, to pass into sailing history. His boat, *Wanderer*, is now on display in the Maritime Museum in Falmouth.

Frank and his wife Margaret were well known for their dinghy cruising, writing a book on the subject and inspiring a generation of enthusiastic dinghy sailors. They were familiar figures on the Norfolk coast for many years. Latterly, after Frank died, Margaret was often to be seen sailing her Wanderer dinghy on Hickling Broad in all weathers.

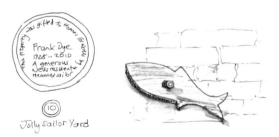

right The Dyes' cottage, number 10 Jolly Sailor Yard, was left to Homes For Wells and this plaque can be seen on the wall outside

far right Fish-shaped wall tie in Jolly Sailor Yard

THE LIFEBOAT *LUCY LAVERS*

The *Lucy Lavers* was restored by the charity Rescue Wooden Boats. She was built as the lifeboat for Aldeburgh in 1940, and soon after her launching she went to help rescue some of the 338,000 Allied Forces from the beach at Dunkirk.

The RNLI (Royal National Lifeboat Institution) was formed in 1824 and the lifeboats were double-ended, pulling boats with up to ten pairs of oars. They had two masts, each with a lugsail.

After her replacement at Aldeburgh by another boat, she was used as a relief lifeboat for Wells, Sheringham, Rhyl and Flanborough, before her conversion to a pilot boat in 1968.

By the time she was eventually rescued by the Dunkirk Little Ships Society, she had worked as a fishing boat, and as a dive and ski boat in Jersey.

She was finally restored in 2010 by Hewitts Boatbuilders at the Rescue Wooden Boats centre in Stiffkey, and went back to Dunkirk, in May 2015, as part of the celebrations for the sixty remaining *Dunkirk Little Ships*.

She now lies in Wells harbour for the summer.

THE DUNKIRK RESCUE

The rescue of the combined forces of British, French and Belgian troops stranded on the beaches at Dunkirk in the Second World War, between 26th May and 4th June 1940, is one of the heroic stories of the War. Trapped on the beach with the German army behind them and the Luftwaffe bombing from above, there seemed no hope for the men of the Allied Forces. But in an extraordinary rescue led by Vice-Admiral Bertram Ramsay and code-named Operation Dynamo, a fleet of naval vessels, supported by small boats from all over the south coast, sailed across the Channel to try to evacuate the troops.

The flag of the Dunkirk Little Ships Society

Ramsay had sent naval officers out to scour the Thames for small boats that could be requisitioned for use, and quickly an enthusiastic response from civilians produced a fleet of nearly 400 small boats which they willingly crossed to Dunkirk, risking their lives to take part in the evacuation.

The large naval ships could not get near the beach, so the small boats were needed to get closer to the shore. The soldiers waded out to be ferried across to the large ships waiting to take them away. All the while German bombs were falling on both the rescue ships and the stranded army alike. The troops crowded onto the decks in order to avoid getting trapped below if they were hit by one of the bombs.

The volunteer boats, known now as the Dunkirk Little Ships, included car ferries, speed boats, Thames boats, lifeboats, fishing boats, and pleasure craft of all kinds. In all, 338,226 men were rescued during the operation, which also saw the loss of 226 vessels, including 170 of the small craft.

THE *ALBATROS*

The Dutch sailing ship *Albatros* has been a well-known sight on the quay at Wells since the 1990s. A two-masted, gaff-rigged cargo ship, she was built in 1899, and traded under sail between Holland and the Baltic, not having an engine installed until 1933.

During the Second World War under her Danish owner, Captain Rasmussen, she helped to rescue dissidents and Jews from Denmark, which was by then occupied by the Nazis, taking them to Sweden which had remained neutral, and smuggling weapons and explosives back to Denmark for the Resistance.

Still trading in 1964, Captain Rasmussen had reduced her sails to a single stay sail, which helps to keep a ship steady at sea, and installed a bigger engine. He retired eventually in 1978 and the Albatros was lying in Copenhagen when she was bought by her present owner, Ton Brouwer, who sailed her back to Holland for restoration in Amsterdam. In 1987 she was

The *Albatros*

recommissioned as a sailing cargo ship and she was the only sailing cargo vessel in northwest Europe.

Between 1990 and 1996 she was a regular visitor to Wells, carrying soybean meal. In 1997 she was licensed to carry passengers, and Greenpeace used her in Holland for two years as a venue for children's education.

The Albatros Project in Wells, formed in 2001, tried to keep her in use for cruises and education but was dissolved four years later, and Ton Brouwer now runs her as a bar and cafe on the quay at Wells. The outline of her rigging against the sky and the gantry of the Old Granary have become a signature of Wells and a reminder of the not so distant days when the harbour would have been alive with ships, sailors and fishermen.

STIFFKEY

Lying on the coast between Morston and Wells, Stiffkey occupies the area of saltmarsh where the Stiffkey River meets the sea. This river was used for the transport of stone from France, via Blakeney, for the building of Walsingham and Binham priories.

Stiffkey remains known now only for the tale of its defrocked vicar and for its cockles known as *Stewkey Blues*. The cockles are stained blue by the local mud. Pots from the extensive Roman potteries at Brampton, near Aylsham, are also recognised by this characteristic blue clay.

HAROLD DAVIDSON (1875–1937)

Harold Davidson was appointed rector of Stiffkey in 1902. He had become very concerned for the prostitutes in London and spent a great deal of time there rescuing 'fallen' women.

Serving for four years in the Great War, he returned home to find his wife pregnant. This finished off his marriage and he spent more and more time with the prostitutes in Soho.

In 1932, when Davidson was in his sixties, a Fleet Street reporter picked up on his apparent misbehaviour and the story of his church trial went worldwide. He was defrocked in Norwich Cathedral on 21st October 1932.

He then joined a circus and spent a year sitting on a barrel proclaiming his innocence, while people paid twopence to see him.

While the circus was in Skegness in 1938, he was taking the part of Daniel in the lion's den, preaching from inside the lions' cage, when the usually docile lion, Freddie, attacked him and Harold died of his injuries a few days later.

Dangerous times…

There is a memorial in Colney Church, just south of Norwich, to a young man who was also eaten by a lion

WILLIAM FADEN (1749–1836)

William Faden, the son of a printer, also called William, was well known as a cartographer, rising to become Royal Geographer to King George III. With a team of assistants he surveyed Norfolk between 1790 and 1794, publishing the first large-scale map of the county in 1797, to a scale of one inch to the mile. Following the Enclosure Act, within fifteen years of its publication, the extensive commons, heaths and warrens had largely disappeared. The entire map has been digitally redrawn and can be seen online, providing a fascinating record of how the county looked at that time.

opposite Faden's map of Norfolk, 1797

THE GLAVEN PORTS:
BLAKENEY,
CLEY,
WIVETON

The River Glaven was shallow and had no tributaries to connect it with major inland settlements, but it was very fast flowing which made it a good river for watermills, and nonetheless it had four ports, which were Blakeney, Cley, Wiveton and the much smaller one of Salthouse which has long since disappeared. Blakeney is sometimes referred to as Snitterly, and there is an unresolved question as to whether Snitterly was a separate settlement from Blakeney or whether it just changed its name at some point.

The process of longshore drift, whereby the currents bring sand and shingle down the coast and the back wash of the incoming tide brings it into the shore, builds up the long spits which are such a feature of the low-lying coast of East Anglia. The shingle gradually builds up, lengthening it westwards, while shifting slowly inland.

Blakeney was an important port in the Middle Ages, protected by the ever-lengthening shingle spit now called Blakeney Point. The coastline looked very different in the Middle Ages when the Glaven Estuary came inland as far as Cley Church. The quay was by the church at Newgate Green, with Wiveton Church across the water on the other side. By the sixteenth century, the spit had grown into a protective arm sheltering the harbour. Both Cley and Blakeney were established ports by the mid-thirteenth century.

In 1223 Blakeney was granted a weekly market and an annual fair on St Nicholas Day, and some thirty years later Cley was also granted a weekly market and later still an annual fair on St Margaret's Day.

In the fourteenth century St Margaret's Church at Cley was rebuilt and the present nave, transepts and aisles date from this period: the church was completed around 1450. The nave and tower of St Nicholas Church at Blakeney underwent reconstruction in the fifteenth century.

A map of the area dated 1586 raises some interesting points. St Margaret's Church at Cley had a spire, not the tower which is there now, and St Nicholas Church at Blakeney did not have the now-familiar lantern tower on the east end. The arm of the Glaven reached as far as Salthouse, which for a time was also a port, until the constant silting up of the channel made navigation impossible. The river divided into two channels at Cley and Blakeney, with two bridges sited further upstream. There is a group of six men at top left who seem to be breaking up a boat, possibly a wreck, and three figures near them who are digging bait or maybe cockling. Just below them are two men fighting with swords, and a figure on a horse is riding from Morston towards Blakeney along the boundary between the marsh and the fields. Blakeney Eye, a small hill of glacial till deposited at the retreat of the last Ice Age, is

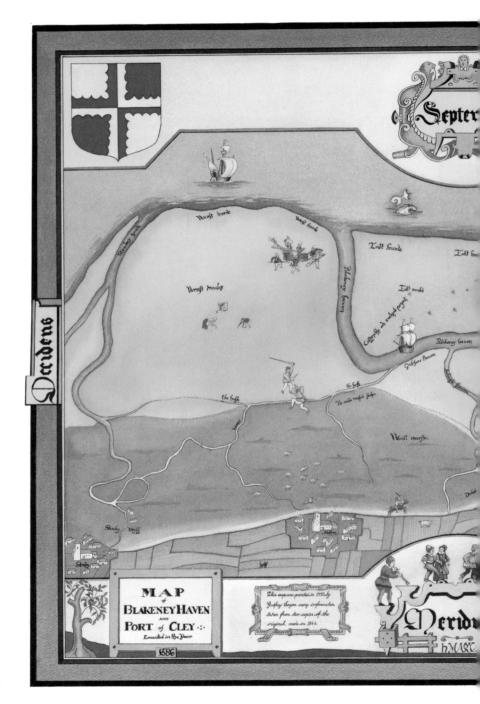

A map, painted by
Godfrey Sayers of
Wiveton, replicating an
original dating from 1586

teeming with rabbits and there is a figure with a long line disappearing into the ground. Could he be catching rabbits with a ferret? Another figure, on the bottom right, is wielding a staff which has the scale of the map drawn on it. He has a pair of dividers at his belt and is wearing a horned mask. This is quite likely to be the map maker, who is thought to be John Derby from Ipswich.

FISHING

The fish caught was mostly cod, ling and orgey – a larger variety of ling which was much prized for its size and its relative rarity. They were usually salted and were a staple of the medieval diet. Surplus fish would probably have gone to Lynn or Yarmouth for distribution through their inland rivers.

By the sixteenth century, most of the fishing boats were going off to fish the coast of Iceland. This change in location was probably due to several factors. The migratory habits of the fish had changed, and the North Sea had its dangers of navigation over the treacherous sandbanks.

In 1516 a charter was granted to Blakeney, giving it the exclusive rights to supply the priories of Binham and Walsingham with fish.

Ling

Cod

Oysters

Extensive beds of oysters were found off Brancaster in the first half of the nineteenth century, and oyster fattening pits were made at Brancaster and Blakeney. By 1870 there were 18 oyster smacks dredging for oysters in Blakeney harbour. The beds were eventually overfished by fishermen from Colchester, and the trade declined.

The last of the Blakeney oyster smacks was a boat called *Pelican*. She was a 25-foot, double-ended cutter with a small cuddy and a large cockpit. She dredged with her owner Ted Buck until 1935.

Mussels

Mussels were raked out of the sand on mussel *scaups* and then boiled in coppers either in the harbour or in the back yards of the fishermen.

The Wells craft were called 'flatbottoms' and the Blakeney ones were 'canoes'. They were usually about 15 feet long and 3 feet wide, with three or four deal clinker planks each side, flat-bottomed with a broad heel at the transom to give buoyancy under large loads. The bottom was usually elm and the frames, or ribs, were of oak. They were rowed or poled and sometimes carried a lugsail as well.

There were still many being used right up to 1950, but now the only one remaining is in the Museum of East Anglian Life in Stowmarket.

THE GREAT FIRE OF CLEY

On the night of September 1st 1612, a fire destroyed 117 buildings in Cley. The town was rebuilt further towards the sea at the position of the current windmill. There was already a settlement there and some quays – an area called Cley Northgate. The area by the church, now Newgate Green, was called Cley Southgate. This move was to save the port when the Glaven was embanked 25 years later.

THE DRAINAGE OF THE MARSHES
AND THE END OF THE GLAVEN PORTS

In 1637 Lord Calthorpe was granted permission to drain the marshes. He brought over the Dutch engineer Jan van Hasenduck to build a bank across the mouth of the River Glaven at Cley, near to where the A149 runs now.

It seems extraordinary today that he was allowed to block the river in this way. Boats could no longer get to Wiveton or to Newgate Green. Cley had by this time been rebuilt after the fire and moved closer to the sea, placing it now to seaward of the new bank, so the port was less affected than Wiveton.

The ensuing protests led to a reversal of the decision, and the embankment was removed, but agriculture would eventually triumph over navigation and even Cley could not remain as a significant port.

This map, based on one made in 1693, shows the approximate positions of Calthorpe's embankment, and the present-day A149

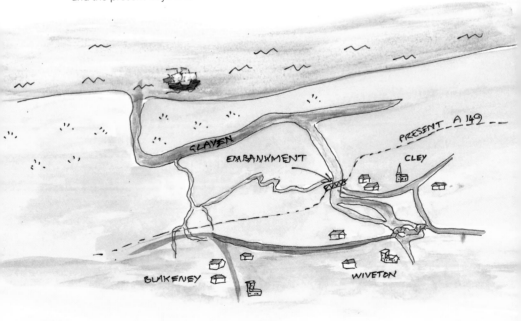

In 1824 the Blakeney and Wiveton Enclosure Act empowered the rebuilding of Calthorpe's bank, with the effect of halving the imports of coal at Cley the following year, and eventually the Custom House at Cley became redundant and its duties were absorbed into Wells.

But, despite these changes, the Glaven ports continued to play a vital part in trade between the North and Sheringham, Cromer and Mundesley.

PIRACY AND SMUGGLING

When fishing was bad, piracy and smuggling thrived. There is a story of how, in 1406, Sir John Prendergast and Robert Bacon from Cromer were running pirate ships. They intercepted and kidnapped James, son of Robert III of Scotland, and took him to London where he was imprisoned by Henry IV in the Tower for twenty years. Two hundred years later, the Spanish King granted *letters of marque* to Henry Carew and Thomas Hubbert, authorising them to seize ships from the Netherlands and to sell their goods. They used north Norfolk as their base.

The Old Custom House at Cley has this wooden frieze above the front door, rather overgrown with creeper at the time of writing this, showing four customs men and an officer with a drawn sword surprising two smugglers unloading a ship onto a pack horse

LETTERS OF MARQUE

A letter of marque was a government licence authorising a privateer to capture enemy vessels during a war. Cruising for prizes with a letter of marque became a lucrative business and was also considered to be patriotic. It was first used by Edward I in 1295.

The system allowed merchant vessels to take prizes without risk of being prosecuted for piracy, and in effect converted a private ship into an auxiliary naval one. The prize had to be brought before an Admiralty Court where it was decided if the letter of marque was valid and if the vessel and its cargo did actually belong to the enemy. If both these conditions were met, the prize was sold at auction and the profits divided between the captain and crew.

CHURCH SHIPS

There is a widespread tradition all over Europe of model ships appearing in churches. A ship resembles both a coffin and a cradle, and this could account for the many superstitious beliefs and customs connected with them. Ship burials are a well-known pre-Christian manifestation of this, and the ship features in many Christian symbols. In the fourth century a bishop's role was described as being like the commander of a great ship.

The roof of a church resembles an upturned ship, and is reflected in the term 'nave', and a mast with its yard arms resembles the cross. Noah's Ark is

This model of a topsail schooner in Cley Church has lost its provenance but is thought to be a ship that foundered off the north Norfolk coast

another common image to be found in carvings and stained glass. Similarly, the compass rose is often represented somewhere in a church; Canterbury Cathedral has one in the floor of the nave.

Some models are probably votive offerings for the souls of men who were lost when their ship went down, or were given in thanks for the safe return of a ship.

One of the earliest records of a church ship is the silver model of Henry III's great ship which he presented to Bromholm Abbey in 1227. Near Bacton on the east coast of Norfolk, the abbey also had a miracle-producing fragment of the True Cross which attracted pilgrims for several hundred years, before finally meeting its fate at the Dissolution.

St Edmund's Church in Southwold has a model of the *Alfred Corry*, the town's nineteenth-century lifeboat.

MEDIEVAL SHIP GRAFFITI

All of the Glaven port churches have medieval graffiti of ships carved into some of their pillars. This is until recently a little studied part of cultural history, partly because of the difficulty of seeing the scratch marks now the pillars have lost their paint, but more and more are being discovered. The Norfolk churches have been well studied but it is likely that medieval graffiti generally are widespread around the country.

The ship graffiti usually appear on the pillars near the chancel and are often adjacent to a side chapel. The reason for their inscription is not yet understood but they were clearly tolerated, if not actually encouraged, as they would have shown up very clearly against the paintwork on the stone, and they were in prominent positions. Subsequent graffiti always respected the existing ones, as they were not scratched away to remove them.

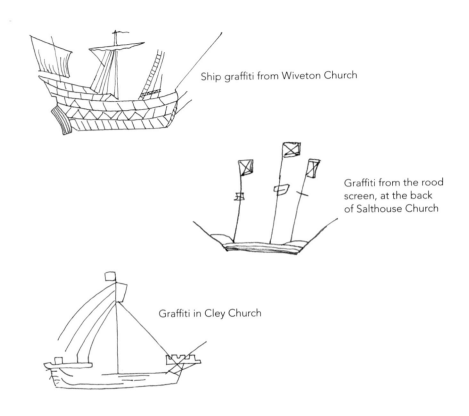

Ship graffiti from Wiveton Church

Graffiti from the rood screen, at the back of Salthouse Church

Graffiti in Cley Church

Various reasons for them have been proposed. As they were often near the side chapel dedicated to St Nicholas, the patron saint of sailors, they could have been offered in hope or in thanks for the safe return of a ship by the sailor's family or the merchant owner. They are usually dated by the design of the ship depicted, and are often quite detailed. Wiveton Church, particularly, has a lot of merchant marks as well as the ships.

Salthouse Church has a great many ships inscribed into the wood of the back of the choir stalls and also several on the back of the rood screen.

Billy Boy

SHIPS

The Newcastle, Hull and London *packets* made regular monthly sailings to those destinations and took passengers as well as goods.

A *Billy Boy* was a type of flat-bottomed, high-sided, apple-bowed ship, not unlike a barge, which developed on the east coast. Her roomy shape allowed her to carry a lot of cargo. She usually carried leeboards, which were short flat planks pivoted to the outside of the hull, one each side, which could be raised or lowered as needed. This compensated for the lack of a keel. The keel would normally prevent a vessel from crabbing sideways if the wind was coming from any direction other than behind.

Billy Boys evolved for beach work up and down the east coast and could be rigged either as a sloop, with one mast, or as a ketch with two. They usually carried some square sails, and can sometimes be seen featured in paintings of the Norwich School.

Most of the Billy Boys were built in Yorkshire and they were said to be the largest clinker-built boats in Europe. The Yorkshire vessels were frequently painted green with a varnished top plank and red rubbing strakes. If the skipper or the owner had died within twelve months, she would be painted blue instead of green. Decks were tarred and sanded for better grip.

The Billy Boy *Bluejacket* remains a well-remembered vessel in Blakeney. She was built at Walsoken in 1860. She was *carvel*-built, that is the planks were flush, not overlapping as in clinker building, and she did not carry leeboards. She was later stripped of her masts and used by Page and Turner, maltsters and merchants of Blakeney, as a lighter in the harbour until 1911. She was then abandoned and lay on the west bank of Morston Creek, her hull eventually rotting on the Morston marshes.

A *clipper* was a type of ship designed for a particular trade and to carry a specialised cargo. They often carried passengers as well, but always with the aim of sailing as fast as was possible. A clipper would carry a vast amount of canvas and was usually driven at maximum speed both by day and night, usually carrying perishable or valuable goods such as tea from China, and commanding very high rates. There were very few clippers built, compared with other trading ships, and they were at their peak between 1845 and 1875, after which they were superseded by steam ships.

SHIP OWNERS

In 1860 thirty vessels were owned by merchants in Cley, some of which were engaged in worldwide trading. It was common for the local traders and merchants to own ships as well, investing in the important business of transporting goods by sea in times when moving things by land was difficult and time-consuming.

John Lee was a miller, maltster and merchant, and owner of Cley Mill in 1819; he had two lighters and shares in five other vessels.

William Cook, a Glandford miller, owned the 168-ton schooner the *Newcastle Packet*.

William Allen, the postmaster at Weybourne and a draper and grocer, owned the 168-ton brig *Elizabeth*.

The Starlings of Blakeney owned three vessels, all commanded by members of the family.

A tea clipper of similar rig to the *Cutty Sark*

RICHARD WOODGET (1845–1928)

Richard Woodget was born in Burnham Norton in 1845 and learned his trade in coasters off the east coast. He became captain of the *Cutty Sark* in 1885, a position he held for ten years. The *Cutty Sark* was built at Dumbarton in 1869 as a clipper for the tea run to China, but by the time Richard Woodget took her command, the tea trade had been largely taken over by steamships and she was now carrying wool from Australia to Britain.

She was often pitched against the *Thermopylae* on the same run but usually out-sailed her. The trip from New South Wales to Dungeness on one occasion took her only 71 days. I was taught to sail in my teens by retired naval commander Bill Smith who, as a young lad from Sydney, had enlisted as a cabin boy on the *Thermopylae* and would relate stories of rounding Cape Horn with the ship driven at full speed in the legendary South Atlantic gales.

In 1895 the *Cutty Sark*'s owner decided to sell her, as steamships were now taking over from sail for the wool run, as they already had for the China tea trade, and she was sold for £2,100 to a Portuguese firm who renamed her the *Ferreira* of Lisbon.

In 1922, when seeking refuge from a storm in Falmouth, Captain Wilfred Dowman – a long admirer of the ship – spotted her, negotiated a price with the Portuguese owner, and bought and subsequently restored her.

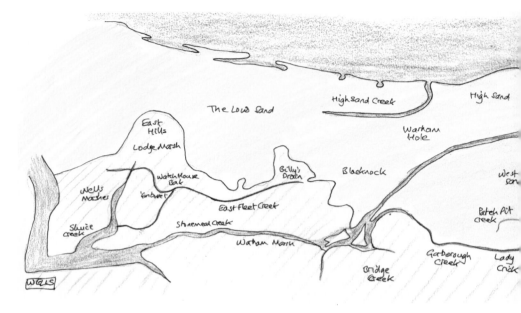

Map of the Blakeney marshes showing Godfrey Sayers' names marked on it

Richard Woodget retired from the sea shortly after leaving the *Cutty Sark* and bought a farm at Burnham Overy which he farmed until his death at 82, but in 1924 he was persuaded to take his old ship under sail from Falmouth round to Fowey, nearly 30 years after relinquishing her command.

He is buried in the churchyard at Burnham Overy, where his grave is marked by a stone anchor paid for by the Shipwrecked Mariners Royal Benevolent Society, of whom Woodget was a staunch supporter.

Annual Sea-blite Suaeda maritima *is a low-growing saltmarsh plant commonly found between the high and low water marks. Shrubby Sea-blite* Suaeda fructicosa *is a fleshy saltmarsh plant found on shingle above the high water mark in the south-east.*

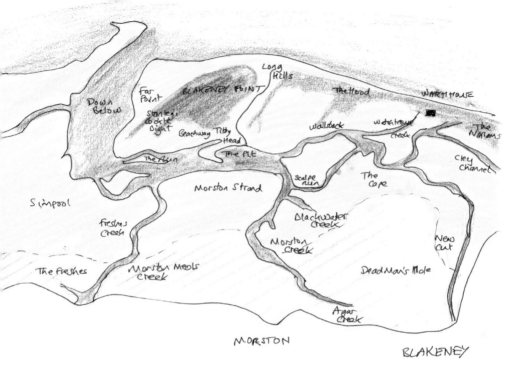

In 2014 Godfrey Sayers published a book on the north Norfolk coast, recording his memories of generations of fishermen from his own family and others. It was illustrated with his own paintings and he records the old names of the marshes which are shown on the map.

Meols is a Viking word for the area between the arable land and that covered by the tide at its highest point. It is colonised by gorse, sea-blite and marsh grasses.

Many Viking words have been incorporated into our language. Here are a few of them relating to places:

bekkr = a stream

bryggr = a jetty

by = a settlement

dik = a ditch

finkel = crooked

gata = a path or road

kirkja = a church

mikill = large

rond = a riverbank

stigr = a path

thorpe = a secondary settlement

toft = a building site

vangr = a field

SHERINGHAM

The Sheringham referred to in the Domesday record is Upper Sheringham, situated about a mile inland; Lower Sheringham, lying on the coast, was just a handful of fishermen's dwellings, but by 1700 it had a population of around one hundred. By 1850, as the fishing industry grew, this number had increased to eight hundred and about one hundred boats were catching fish, lobsters and crabs.

The town grew rapidly during the nineteenth century, with the population rising to 4,000 with the coming of the railway. This had two important effects on the little town. It gave the fishermen access to the London markets for their lobsters and crabs, and Sheringham began a new career as a popular seaside resort.

The crab boats were known as *shannocks*, also a nickname for the Sheringham fishermen. The boats were double-ended, that is pointed at both ends, about 18 feet in length and 7 feet in width. The planks were usually made of elm, oak, larch or pine. They were rigged as single-masted *dipping lugs* with the sails dressed

Sheringham Crabber or 'Shannock'

with cutch, a solution of boiled catechu gum which helped to preserve the sailcloth, giving the sails a black colour.

Three pairs of oars were passed right through the oar ports, which were opposing holes in the top plank, known as the *orrucks*. The stout ash oars were also used as handles for lifting the boats.

There being no harbour, the boats were launched from the beach, and in bad weather the men could often drown only a few yards from the shore while trying to beach the boats after a fishing trip. There was no lifeboat, so Miss Ann Gurney of Northrepps Cottage, Sidestrand, operated her own team of fishermen-lifesavers, providing a pulling boat and equipment in the early nineteenth century.

THE UPCHER FAMILY AND THE SHERINGHAM LIFEBOATS

In 1838 the widow of Abbot Upcher (who had earlier bought the Sheringham Estate in 1812 and subsequently built Sheringham Hall) paid to have another lifeboat built, named 'Augusta' after her youngest child who had died two years earlier. The *Augusta* was built by Robert Sunman, a local boat-builder

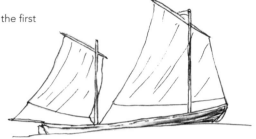

A boat with a dipping lugsail on the first mast and a standing lug on the second mast

opposite Green crab (left) and purple crab (right)

and wheelwright, who built a pulling boat with sixteen oars and costing £150. She was 33 feet 6 inches long and 10 feet 2 inches in the beam, and had a *dipping lugsail*. She was used for 56 years and saved many lives.

The Upchers' son Henry Ramey Upcher took a close interest in the fishermen and encouraged the building of larger decked boats which were safer to operate. He advanced the money for each boat and then was paid back from the profits from the fishing.

This was the time of the Sheringham 'great boats' which had two, sometimes three masts, and were mostly built at Great Yarmouth from about 1830. They were similar to the Yarmouth luggers, with a large dipping lugsail at the main mast and a small standing lug at the mizzen. By the 1870s the large dipping lugsail on the main mast had been replaced by a standing lug.

The bottom forward corner of the dipping lugsail was secured by a rope to the bow, which meant that each time the boat tacked the crew had to undo the line and dip the long spar along its top edge around to the other side of the mast, before securing the rope again. This could be dangerous in strong winds. The standing lug was much easier, as its leading corner was permanently secured to the foot of the mast, removing the need for someone to wrestle with the spar.

In these great boats, the Sheringham fishermen would sail off in the summer to longline for cod off Grimsby, using crab boats on the deck for

working the lines. From April to July they would fish for crab off the Yorkshire coast using crab pots and would bring back live crabs to replenish the stocks at home. The light brown crabs at Sheringham are still called *yorkshiremen*.

The great boats fished for herring from Scarborough to Yarmouth during the herring season, and were laid up at Blakeney or Yarmouth for the winter. Sheringham fishermen settled in Grimsby and also in Whitstable where they used their crab boats for fishing for whelks.

A NEW LIFEBOAT

In 1893, Caroline Upcher, the widow of Henry Ramey Upcher, called a meeting of fishermen with a view to replacing the *Augusta*. It was decided that the new boat would be wider in the beam and have fastenings of copper rather than the iron nails which had caused nail sickness in the older boat. This new lifeboat was built by another local firm of boat-builders, the Emery family – Louis and his son Robert, with help from his brothers – and was named the *Henry Ramey Upcher*.

By this time the RNLI was working alongside the Upchers and supplied another lifeboat, the *William Bennet* and later the *JC Madge*, the latter being the new 'Liverpool' design with an engine, arriving at Sheringham in 1904.

The *Henry Ramey Upcher* was launched fifty times and saved over two hundred lives before finally being laid up in 1935. She can be seen at the Sheringham Lifeboat Museum along with the *JC Madge*.

LIFEBOAT STATIONS

In 1866 Henry Upcher gave some land on the East Cliff to the RNLI to build a lifeboat station. The building had the addition of a first floor for a reading room for sailors, for relaxation and education. The money for this was raised by public subscription.

However, the approach to the sea from here was always problematical and the gangway was often swept away during gales, leading to frequent and expensive repairs. This led to another boat house being built at Old Hythe in 1904, of which just a few bricks remain now on the beach.

The first RNLI lifeboat station was extensively rebuilt at the Millennium and now, named the Oddfellow's Hall, sits on Lifeboat Plain and is used for the community. Sheringham now just has an inshore inflatable lifeboat, and a purpose-built Lifeboat Museum, where some lifeboats can still be seen.

Detail from John Craske's embroidery 'Panorama of the North Norfolk Coast'

In 2012 there were fifty commercial fishermen fishing on the north Norfolk beaches. Most boats have moved to Cromer where the beach is easier for launching, and the boats are mostly fibreglass skiffs worked single-handed with powerful outboard motors.

JOHN CRASKE (1881–1943)

John Craske was born in Sheringham into a fishing family. He suffered from what was probably a form of psychotic nervous depression which eventually saw him in an asylum after having a relapse during military training in 1917. His devoted wife rescued him and looked after him for the rest of her life.

They had moved to Dereham, but a wise doctor recommended the benefits of being near the sea, so they rented houses first in Blakeney, where they had a small sailing boat, and later in Hemsby, further down the coast.

John had started to paint scenes of the coast and fishing boats on any piece of wood or cardboard he could lay his hands on. When he eventually became bedridden, he embroidered these scenes instead, using part of a deckchair as a frame.

His paintings and embroideries were spotted by the poet Valentine Ackland, who bought a painting from him, and as a result of this his work sold in London. John Betjeman and Peter Pears were among his admirers, and he recently had more exposure with two of his pieces in the 'Masterpieces' exhibition at the Sainsbury Centre in Norwich in 2013, and with the publication of his biography *Threads* by Julia Blackburn in 2015.

'A String of Herring' painting

CROMER

Cromer was an inland village until the sea encroached, destroying the coastal settlement of Shipden which was lost in 1300. This now lies under the sea north of Cromer, which now finds itself on the coast. In 1888 the Yarmouth paddle tug *Victoria* went aground off the coast at Cromer and was wrecked there, reputedly by hitting the top of the old church tower of Shipden.

Cromer has no harbour, so cargoes were regularly landed on the beach, as they were further down the coast at Bacton and Mundesley. Colliers unloaded their coal from Yorkshire into horse-drawn carts on the beach during the summer months. During the winter the boats were laid up in Lowestoft or in one of the Glaven ports of Cley, Wiveton or Blakeney.

The railway eventually took over the transport of coal and the last cargo was landed by the two-masted brigantine *Ellis* in 1877. But the railway opened up access to Cromer for holidaymakers, and its fortunes changed as it became a fashionable bathing resort.

THE LIGHTHOUSE

Edward Bowell was granted Letters Patent by George I and a lease by Trinity House in 1719 allowing him to burn a light at the Cromer lighthouse tower.

This was a coal fire in a glazed lantern. When it changed to oil in 1792, it was given the first rotating lantern, enabling it to flash, and thus it could be distinguished from other lights.

The owners of lighthouses were able to charge a due from each passing ship, which gave the incentive for the building of many such lights. But in 1795 Trinity House declined to renew the licence and bought the lighthouse from Edward Bowell. Two major cliff falls in 1825 and 1832 meant its position came under threat and a new one was built further inland, coming into service in 1833.

LIFEBOATS

An advertisement in the *Norwich Mercury* in 1804 arranged a meeting for people interested in encouraging a lifeboat to be stationed at Cromer. This resulted in a boat paid for by public subscription, and then in 1823, Lord Suffield of Gunton, together with Thomas Coke of Holkham and the Vice-Admiral of the Coast, Edmond Wodehouse, set up the first county life-saving association in Britain. The Norfolk Association for Saving the Lives of Shipwrecked Mariners established lifeboat stations at Yarmouth, Caister,

Winterton, Bacton, Blakeney, Wells, Brancaster and Hunstanton. It operated the county's lifeboat service until being taken over by the RNLI in 1858.

In 1894 the young Henry Blogg joined the lifeboat crew of the pulling boat, the *Benjamin Cabbell*. He was to become the most highly decorated lifeboatman of all time.

HENRY BLOGG (1876–1954)

'The greatest lifeboatman that ever lived.'

Henry joined the lifeboat crew in 1894, at the age of eighteen, retiring in 1947 at the age of seventy-one. He served for fifty-three years as a lifeboat-man, thirty-eight of those years as coxswain, and saw the transition from sail and oar to the petrol and then to the diesel engine.

His bravery and leadership qualities were so valued that the RNLI allowed him to continue service well beyond the usual retirement age. His hallmark was the iron will which drove him on in situations where other brave

men would have given up. He remains the most highly decorated lifeboatman of all time, and the stories of his rescues are extraordinary.

A quiet, reserved man he fished in the winter and hired out deckchairs to holiday-makers in the summer months. It was expected that the local fishermen would join the lifeboat crew at the age of eighteen and generations of the fishing families fol-lowed this tradition.

Henry Blogg

He married Ann in 1901 and they lost their son aged only eighteen months and later their daughter Queenie when she was in her twenties.

When he first joined the crew, the lifeboat was a pulling boat, the *Benjamin Cabbell*. She was powered by fourteen oars and a single dipping lugsail.

She was replaced by the *Louisa Heartwell*, first launched in 1917, by which time Henry Blogg was the coxswain.

In the Great War he was given dispensation from the services, as his skills as a lifeboatman were needed in a time when the convoys of merchant ships carrying essential supplies to Great Britain were constant prey to German U-boats in the North Sea. Most of the crew were older men unable to fight in the War.

SOME OF HENRY BLOGG'S INSPIRING RESCUES

Some of Henry Blogg's rescues as a lifeboatman have been recorded in a book by Mick Bensley, which I read in the public library in Wells with a feeling of increasing awe and respect for this man who combined courage and superb seamanship with the ability to inspire the men around him to achieve some of the most daring and brilliant rescues ever carried out by the lifeboat service.

The rescue of the SS *Pyrin* of Piraeus and the SS *Fernebo*, a Swedish steamer from Gothenburg, in December 1917

On this night, there was a force 7–9 NNE gale blowing with heavy seas, hail and snow squalls. The lifeboat *Louisa Heartwell* was launched at 11.40am. The combination of a heavy onshore gale and a shallow bank over which the boat had to be taken to get to the deep water made launching particularly difficult, but with the help of the many soldiers who were stationed at Cromer at the time, some of whom waded into the water up to their waists, she finally put to sea.

Struggling to get to a position where she could set her sails, and having narrowly missed drifting onto the end of the pier, she managed to reach the

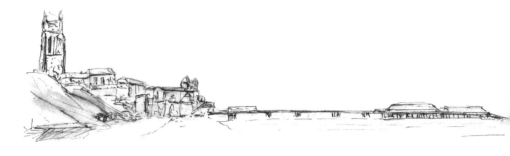

Cromer pier

stricken ship by 2pm and landed the crew safely at Cromer an hour later. Just as she reached the shore, an explosion was heard as another ship, the SS *Fernebo*, hit a mine, bursting one of her boilers. Having heard that both the Sheringham and the Palling lifeboats were unable to launch due to the worsening conditions, the Cromer crew, despite their recent exhausting rescue, decided to launch again but were constantly beaten back as they tried to row her out. During this time, a small boat from the *Fernebo* made it towards the shore where she capsized, and again the local people, soldiers and sailors waded into the huge breakers to form a human chain to pull them all to safety.

Meantime, the steamer had broken in two, but with a load of timber on board the two sections remained afloat and started to drift apart. Rockets were fired again and again, unsuccessfully, to get a line onto the wreck and at 9.30pm the Cromer crew decided to try again. Time after time they were beaten back by the gale and the seas, losing three oars and breaking five more. The army searchlights offered glimpses of her heroic efforts, sometimes seeing her appear to stand on end and sometimes disappearing into the foam altogether. Making another attempt at 11pm, Henry Blogg noticed a point on the beach where the tide had begun to make a current which swept out almost to the ship. Having found some replacement oars by this time, they at last succeeded, and she reached the wreck 35 minutes later, bringing all eleven of her crew back to safety. She finally reached the shore at 1.30am. The average age of the crew was fifty and the oldest man was seventy.

Henry was awarded his first gold medal for this, and the second coxswain a silver medal. The RNLI struck a bronze medal specially for all the crew.

The *Louisa Heartwell* was replaced by the *H F Bailey*, which is the longest serving of all the lifeboats. She was launched 387 times.

The rescue of SS *Georgia* of Rotterdam on 21st/22nd November 1927

The *Georgia*, a large oil tanker, was spotted at 2pm from the cliff by two fishermen. She was sinking in a great gale. The *H F Bailey* was launched but found no sign of life on board. Realising the *Georgia* was a danger to shipping, the *H F Bailey* stood by until morning.

The old sailing lifeboat, the *Louisa Heartwell*, then took over the standby as a message came through that the ship had broken in two and that only the stern section was off Cromer, the bow section having gone aground on the Haisboro Sands with fifteen men on board.

The Gorleston lifeboat and three passing steamers attempted to help but efforts to reach her failed, and the crew were crouched in the foc'sle having had no food or water for a good forty hours. Shortly after 4pm, the *H F Bailey* arrived just as the ship burst her tanks and thousands of tons of oil spilled onto the sea, calming it down a little. The skipper of the tanker ordered his men to line up on the bridge, the youngest first and himself last.

The *H F Bailey* sustained severe damage to her sternpost, rudder and starboard side but managed to get a line across to make her fast, while the crew jumped into the sea one by one. The lifeboat nearly capsized after rescuing the men, when the seas drove the boat onto the wrecked ship's bulwarks, but the quick-thinking engineer reversed his engines and there was just enough water around the propeller for the boat to clear the ship. She reached Gorleston at 6.25pm, having been on continual service for twenty-eight hours.

Henry Blogg received a second clasp to his gold medal and the crew received the bronze medal.

The rescue of the SS *Monte Nevosa* on 14th–16th October 1932

The *Monte Nevosa* ran aground on the Haisboro Sands in a north-westerly gale and the *H F Bailey* was launched at 9.30am in response to a request to stand by while two tugs tried to tow her off. But by 5am the next morning they had to abandon their attempts, as their lines had broken, and the lifeboat was asked to take off the crew.

Twenty-nine men were taken off but the four officers refused to leave the ship. The lifeboat took the crew to Yarmouth and, after refuelling and changing into dry clothing, returned for the officers, who still refused their assistance.

Retiring to Yarmouth again they made yet another return journey at 5am, only to find that the four men had gone in their boat but had left two dogs behind. The smaller of the dogs could not be caught but they managed to rescue the St Bernard and, naming it Monte, it became Henry Blogg's constant companion.

Henry Blogg and Monte became a familiar sight to holidaymakers renting their deckchairs from Henry on the beach at Cromer during the summer months.

The rescue of the *Sepoy* in December 1933

When the Thames sailing barge, the *Sepoy*, set off on her passage in December 1933 she could have had little idea of the fate that was awaiting her. The shallow waters of the east coast became even more treacherous with an onshore wind, and a strong easterly gale blew up, driving her onto the notorious Haisboro Sands.

It was 13th December and Henry Blogg was returning from Yarmouth, having been to the aid of another barge, the *Gurney*, at 4.30 that morning. By this time the old pulling lifeboat had been replaced by the *H F Bailey*, powered by a petrol

This photograph, taken from the shore, shows the stricken barge aground on the sands and the lifeboat approaching her with her oars clearly visible as they struggle to get near her. The two men can be seen clinging to the rigging by the mast.

engine. The strength of the easterly gale had made it impossible to launch the *Alexandra* lifeboat from Cromer beach despite repeated attempts from 8.30am until 1.30pm, and eventually the Gorleston lifeboat managed to get a message to the *H F Bailey*.

They found the barge stranded not 200 yards from the shore, with her decks under water. The heavy seas made the attempts to come alongside impossible and Henry decided to risk driving the lifeboat onto her flooding decks. He ran her straight over the deck, snatching the mate, and then a second time to grab the skipper.

Henry Blogg was awarded a clasp to his silver medal and the crew received thanks from the RNLI on vellum.

opposite Henry Blogg and Monte

HAPPISBURGH
AND THE LOST VILLAGES
OF THE EAST COAST

The coast from Cromer down to Great Yarmouth has lost a number of villages over the centuries. The Domesday book records at least fourteen villages which are no longer here. The map overleaf shows their approximate positions, with the names as recorded in the Domesday Record. Shipden, off the coast at Cromer, and Eccles-Juxta-Mare are the most well known. The rest lie unexplored under the sea. Records from the time show that the storminess of the North Sea increased during the thirteenth and fourteenth centuries, and the sea levels were rising. This, combined with the low-lying land on which these villages were built, made their existence precarious, and much land and many lives were lost during this period, which also led to the flooding of the old peat diggings which made the Norfolk Broads.

As recently as the Millennium, it was within living memory that people could recall another coast road on the seaward side of the existing one, with fields beyond. This road is now gone, and the flooding process still continues. Poor maintenance of the dunes led to a major breach in the night of 31st January 1953, when seven people from Sea Palling drowned. In 1986 the sea wall was extended, and in 1995 nine barrier reefs were constructed along the shore. The fiercest of the storms were called *rages* and it was during these rages that large areas of land were lost, often in one night.

ECCLES-JUXTA-MARE

Excavation of the remains of the village has built up a better understanding of Eccles-Juxta-Mare. Built on low-lying land, Eccles was a prosperous fishing village in Saxon times, but by the twelfth century sea levels were starting to rise. With the increasing frequency of the North Sea storms, much of the settlement had been destroyed by the late sixteenth century. There were three recorded breaches by the sea in 1570, during which hundreds of acres were lost to the sea. The church was ruined, leaving only the tower, which stood for another 325 years before finally toppling into the sea in January 1895. During another terrible storm in 1604, two thousand acres were inundated by the sea and sixty-six houses swept away.

In 1840 Charles Lyell visited Eccles and, noting the position of the tower in the dunes, realised it could be used to monitor coastal erosion. Twenty years later it would be on the foreshore, and was recorded in an engraving by Hodgson, and several photographs, notably by Fitt, a Norwich photographer, in 1890. Lyell put this observation into his famous book *The Principles of Geology*, and ever since then, geologists have used Eccles as a *type locality* to study the effects of coastal erosion.

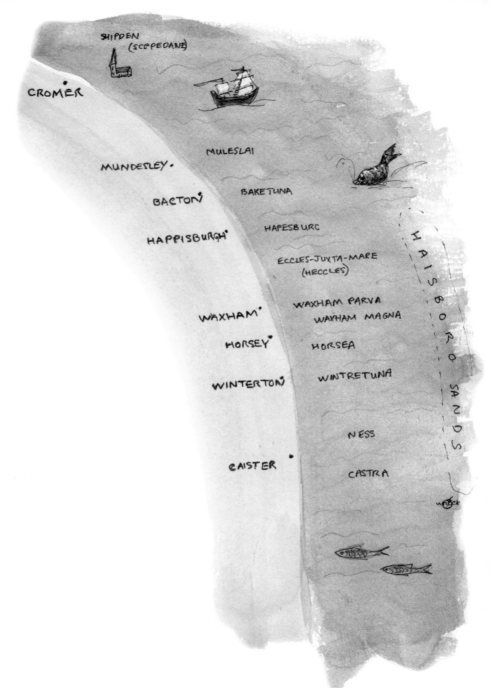

SHIPDEN
(SCEPEDANE)

CROMER

MUNDESLEY.

MULESLAI

BACTON

BAKETUNA

HAPPISBURGH

HAPESBURC

ECCLES-JUXTA-MARE
(HECCLES)

WAXHAM

WAXHAM PARVA
WAXHAM MAGNA

HORSEY

HORSEA

WINTERTON

WINTRETUNA

NESS

CAISTER

CASTRA

HAISBORO SANDS

HMS *INVINCIBLE*
AND THE MYSTERIOUS MOUND
IN HAPPISBURGH CHURCHYARD

One day in 1988 a small team of builders were at work digging a drainage trench in Happisburgh churchyard in order to disperse rainwater from the roof of the church. As their digger started to move the earth away from a mound on the north side of the church, some bones began to appear; the builders had found an unmarked grave. In due course the remains of a total of 119 bodies were revealed in the mound.

It had been handed down for many years by word of mouth in the village that a naval ship, on its way to join the fleet in the Baltic, had been wrecked off the coast nearby, with great loss of life, and that the bodies had been buried in a large communal grave, the location of which had long since been forgotten.

HMS *Invincible* was a third rate, 74-gun Ship-of-the-Line sailing from the naval dockyard at Chatham on the Thames, via Great Yarmouth to pick up victuals, to the Baltic where she was due to join the fleet under the command of the Admirals Hyde-Parker and Nelson, and ultimately to take part in the Battle of Copenhagen. She had a pilot on board to assist with the tricky navigation of the channel between the two sandbanks of the Haisboro Sands and Hammond's Knoll which lay a little further to the east, but, despite all efforts, the combination of a strong ebb tide and a freshening wind drove the ship onto the Hammond's Knoll Sands, where she began to take water. Lightening her load, first by jettisoning some of the provisions and then by cutting her masts away, she managed to float free at high water, but, having lost her rudder, she soon struck the sandbar yet again.

The firing of her guns as a distress signal soon brought the *Nancy*, a local cod fishing smack, to her assistance and the youngest of the crew were taken off. The Invincible lowered her boats but all of them were swept away, apart from one launch which was later to be picked up by a passing collier.

Seven years after the Invincible *went down, the Burial of Persons Drowned At Sea Act 1808 was passed in Parliament to ensure that all bodies found drowned at sea should have a Christian burial in consecrated ground*

It was dark by now and the Nancy stood by hoping to take the remaining crew off at first light; but, as dawn broke, the ship went down. In all, 190 men had been rescued, some of whom were to die later from their injuries and exposure.

For days following, bodies continued to be washed up along the shore and were brought by carts to Happisburgh Church, where a communal grave was dug for them on the glebeland between the churchyard and the cliff; and there they remained until 1988 when the drainage trench was dug. By this time the glebeland had become incorporated into the churchyard and no-one had thought about the mound in the grass to one side of the church.

Ten years after its secret was revealed, in 1998, the Parochial Church Council contacted the Commander of the present-day HMS *Invincible*. He agreed to collaborate in commissioning a memorial stone and in due course a service was held, attended by eight of the present Ship's Company, their Second-in-Command, their Chaplain and a descendant of John Rennie, the captain of the original ship, who had drowned before he could be rescued.

Within sight of Hammond's Knoll, the bugle sounded the Last Post and Reveille and the memorial stone was dedicated to the men who lost their lives that fateful night in 1801. It can be found lying in the churchyard between the church and the sea.

SHIPS, FRIGATES AND NAVAL RATINGS

Readers of Hornblower and the Patrick O'Brian books about Jack Aubrey and Stephen Maturin will be familiar with the terms 'third rate Ship-of-the-Line', 'sloops and frigates' and 'guns and carronades'. But what exactly do these terms mean?

The rating system of the ships of the Royal Navy changed several times between the sixteenth and nineteenth centuries, but during the Napoleonic Wars, about which both C. S. Forester and Patrick O'Brian were writing, a *Ship-of-the-Line* was a ship that was powerful enough to stand in the battle line and to both give and take massive broadsides. Battles at sea were usually fought between two ships which manoeuvred into a position where they could present the maximum number of guns to bear on the enemy. As their artillery disabled the opposing vessels, they would come close enough to board and continue the fight with hand weapons, while snipers fired muskets from vantage points in the rigging.

A *first* and *second* rated ship had three gun-decks carrying upwards of 90 guns.

A *third* rated ship had between 64 and 80 guns, and had either two or three gun-decks.

A *fourth* rated ship had 50–60 guns over two decks, but after the mid-eighteenth century was no longer regarded as big enough for Ship-of-the-Line status and was, confusingly, thereafter referred to as a *frigate*.

The guns referred to were fixed cannons, that is to say they were fixed to wooden, wheeled gun carriages. Smaller lighter guns, attached to wooden slides, were called carronades; *and finally, the terms* 28 *or* 32 pounder *referred to the weight of the cannonballs which they fired.*

This was confusing because, at around the same time, a new class of ship was being built – the *frigate*. This smaller, lighter vessel carried between 28 and 32 guns on her main deck but the second, lower, deck had no gunports due to the risk of taking in seas, the lower deck being closer to the water than on the bigger ships. Frigates were used mainly for carrying dispatches, blockading ports and escorting convoys.

The *post-ship* was smaller still, with 20–24 guns, but still required a post-captain as commander, unlike the even smaller *sloop-of-war* carrying 16–18 guns, and the *gun brigs, cutters* and *schooners* which, carrying only 4–14 guns, could be commanded by a lower-ranking officer such as a lieutenant or sometimes a midshipman.

These ships suffered serious amounts of damage during an engagement with the enemy, the heavy artillery pounding away at close quarters. The ship's carpenter was a key figure in carrying out running repairs on the wooden hull, and the riggers and sailmakers had to improvise with what they stored on board until a proper refit could be carried out at a dockyard. Spare masts were either carried on board or the damaged mast was 'jury rigged' to get the ship back to a port.

The degree of self-reliance and sheer skill which the men on all these ships displayed is extraordinary, to say nothing of the ability of the sailing master to sail a damaged vessel safely back to land and the leadership needed by the captain to hold it all together.

Underwater holes in the hull were sealed by fothering *a sail over the damaged area underneath the ship*

GREAT YARMOUTH

Great Yarmouth began life as a sandbank which gradually built up between 800 and 1000 AD. During the ensuing warm period for the next five hundred years, it emerged from the sea as an island and became populated by fishermen.

From 1500 until 1700 there was a 'Little Ice Age', with repeated storms and poor harvests, and during this time, for reasons which remain disputed, the herring moved their spawning ground out of the Baltic and into the North Sea. 1703 saw the greatest storm the east coast has ever known, and most of the four hundred ships in the Yarmouth Roads were lost. In 1791, a severe flood threw up the shingle bank at Waxham and at Horsey, which remains to this day.

Although today Yarmouth's glory is largely forgotten, it still has the largest open market in the country, the oldest civic building in the country, the oldest football stand and the biggest parish church in Britain. It has the second most complete town wall in the country, became the world's largest herring fishery, and by the turn of the twentieth century it had a leading ship-building industry.

The geography of Great Yarmouth can be a little confusing due to the configuration of the River Bure and Breydon Water, the body of water seen from the bridge as you drive into the town. The River Bure flows southwards into Breydon, running parallel and very close to the coast. It then continues south on the inside of the spit of land on which Yarmouth is built. The spit is fairly narrow so Yarmouth has two parallel waterfronts, one along the river and one by the sea.

TIMELINE

1262
A dwelling built a few years earlier becomes the Tolhouse, the tol being the tax on the sale of herring

1340
The Battle of Sluys was won. Yarmouth provided most of the ships for the King's navy, and Edward III halves his royal coat of arms with that of the town.

1357
The Statute of Herring requires a 'last' to be 10,000 fish

1386
The Dutchman William Beukels finds a way of curing fish by removing the gills and gut before salting the fish. This meant that the fishing boats no longer needed to return to port each day to land their catch.

1400–1500
The Dutch develop drift net fishing

1566
Joas Johnson comes from Holland to find a solution to the problem of the silting up of the harbour

1586
The Dutch arrive in Yarmouth to escape religious persecution, bringing with them their larger fishing boat – the herring buss – and the drift net

1590
The port prospers and is virtually rebuilt

THE SEVENTH HAVEN

The Haven (Great Yarmouth harbour) had undergone many changes since first being dug out in 1346, well down the sandy spit south of Gorleston. Persistently silting up, five further entrances, all closer to Yarmouth town, were successively dug until the final one built between 1536 and 1613, partly under the direction of Joas Johnson, which is still in use today.

1670

The Port and Haven Commissioners are set up

1800

The Dutch herring buss is becoming superseded by the two-masted lugger. Admiral Nelson is granted the Freedom of the Town. He sails to the Baltic from Yarmouth in the following year to win the Battle of Copenhagen.

1807

Captain George Manby invents his life-saving apparatus

1819

The Nelson Monument on the South Denes is built, designed by William Wilkins. When the town surveyor, Thomas Sutton, climbed the stairway to inspect the works, he was suddenly taken ill and died on the spot.

THE PORT AND HAVEN COMMISSION of 1670 was an Act of Parliament giving the Commission the right to tax all imports, except for the herring, and to use the dues for the maintenance and improvements of the harbour.

1845

A circus clown went down the river in a barrel drawn by several geese, watched by crowds on the suspension bridge, which gave way, drowning eighty people

1850

By now there are sixty curing houses in the town and shrimping becomes very profitable due to the large numbers of holidaymakers coming to Yarmouth with the arrival of the railway

1870

Six hundred men are now employed in ship-building and the associated trades

1900

Steam drifters are now replacing the sailing luggers

A SAILOR'S STRIKE in 1851 ended in riots on the Quay which were put down by soldiers from Norwich. The sailors, however, were given a rise in wages.

THE FREE HERRING FAIR

As Yarmouth grew in size, more and more merchants, including many from France, Holland, Italy and Scandinavia, began to make the annual trek to the town developing on its sandbank and soon this annual gathering developed into one of the great fairs of medieval Europe.

The Fair was held for the forty days from Michaelmas to Martinmas. The huge influx of people made keeping order difficult, and the Crown granted the right to men from the Cinque Ports to appoint two bailiffs for the duration of the Fair.

As Yarmouth began to emerge as a small town, rivalry began to break out between the local fishermen and the men from the Cinque Ports of Sandwich, Dover, Hastings, Romney and Hythe, who had been fishing off Yarmouth for many years. The Cinque Ports supplied the King with ships, before the Royal Navy was established, but they also claimed the right to make laws regarding the fishery off Yarmouth.

When Yarmouth was later granted its charter by King John, giving the burgesses of the town the right to hold their own courts, the fact that the Barons of Hastings also had this right was overlooked and so the resentment continued, with fights breaking out whenever the two sides met. In 1277 the grievances of both parties were heard in London and the King ordained that the Yarmouth bailiffs should share the administration of the Herring Fair equally with those of the Cinque Ports.

This peace, however, was never really honoured and fights continued, until in 1297 a battle ensued between the fleet from Yarmouth and that from Cinque Ports, which were escorting the King of Flanders. Twenty-five ships were sunk and two hundred men died. As this represented practically the entire naval fleet, it put national security at risk.

But the Cinque Ports, which by this time had grown to seven, incorporating Rye and Winchelsea, were in decline due to both coastal erosion and the silting up of their harbours and by 1340, at the Battle of Sluys, Yarmouth provided the King's Navy with more ships than the entire Cinque Ports combined. In recognition of this, the first victory of the newly formed King's Navy, King Edward III halved his royal coat of arms with that of the town.

above left Plate of bloaters
above right Herring ready for smoking on a speet

opposite The coat of arms for Great Yarmouth.
The royal lions now have the tails of the herring.

View from the South Quay looking over the river to Southtown

THE ROWS

As in many medieval towns the majority of dwellings were built within the town walls and, of necessity, very close together.

In Yarmouth the system of The Rows was developed, with the closely packed houses separated by narrow streets leading down to the river. There were similar street patterns to this in Kirkwall in Orkney, Birka in Sweden, and parts of Hanseatic Bergen in Norway. It made for easy access to the river and also allowed any floodwater to drain away quickly.

Incendiary bombs in the Second World War gutted most of the houses in The Rows and they were later pulled down, but a few still remain.

The Rows were too narrow for ordinary transport, so the *troll cart* was designed – a small cart with its wheels on a short axle under the body of the carriage, making the width of the entire cart no more than 3 feet.

There were 145 Rows, all of which had names until 1804 when they were given numbers

THE HERRING FISHERY

Herring are *pelagic* fish, meaning that they feed on the plankton in the upper layers of the sea, coming to the surface to feed at dusk.

A herring matures at the age of three or four years and lives for approximately ten years. They migrate around the coast and in early summer are to be found off the west coast of Scotland; in mid-summer they move north around the Shetland Islands and then west along the north coast, coming down the east coast of England and arriving at Great Yarmouth in August where they breed, until they depart in December.

The Smith Knoll is a ridge on the seabed 25 miles off the coast at Yarmouth and is the world's premier breeding ground for herring.

The Dutch

In 1586 Elizabeth I granted thirty Dutch fishing families the right to live and work in Yarmouth to escape religious persecution. They brought with them the drift net and the *buss* (shown below), which was the name of their seventy-foot, high-sided, wide-decked fishing boats.

Some years earlier similar rights had been granted for thirty master weavers, spinners and dyers to come from the Low Countries. Norwich had been renowned for its manufacture of English worsted, but as fashions changed, the more luxurious fabrics being produced in the Low Countries were becoming very popular and the textile industry in Norwich began to decline. The forward-thinking Mayor of Norwich at that time, a cloth merchant by the name of Thomas Sotherton, petitioned the Queen via the Duke of Norfolk, that Letters Patent should be granted to Dutch and Flemish craftsmen, allowing them to live and work in Norwich to pass on their new methods of cloth production in the hope that it would revitalise Norwich's textiles and make it a competitive industry once more. Only too glad of the chance to get away from the oppression of the Calvinist faith by the Catholic Spanish King Philip II who ruled the Low Countries at the time, thirty craftsmen with their families came to Norwich in 1565. They were known as *The Strangers* and their influence was to secure the place of Norwich in the textile trade for another two centuries. But that is another story.

Dutch prosperity and its development as a powerful maritime nation was largely due to the herring which they had been catching in the North Sea since the thirteenth century. Their fishery continued to develop throughout the fifteenth and sixteenth centuries as they extended their fishing into the North Sea.

Each year the 21st September was known locally as 'Dutch Sunday' on account of the celebration of rituals in preparation for the fishing season when the Dutch fished from the sea off Yarmouth until St Catherine's Day on 25th November. The highly profitable Dutch fishery was a source of local envy.

Drifting for herring

Drifting involved shooting a long line of nets from the boat to form a long vertical curtain suspended from floats while the boats drifted slowly with the tide waiting for the herring to rise to the surface to feed, when the fish would swim into the nets to become entrapped by their gills.

The nets were then hauled in and shaken to release the entrapped fish onto the deck from where they could be shovelled into the hold. They were held in large containers, closely packed to avoid damage to the scales and also to control where the weight was distributed to maintain even ballast.

Landing the catch

The boats would then race back to shore where they would beach and the catch would be landed in willow baskets swung ashore from a yard arm. They would be loaded into troll carts drawn by horses.

The Statute of Herring 1357, brought in to regulate trade in the fishing industry, required the measure of a *last* to be 10,000 fish. Later the measure became a *barrel* which was 1,100 fish, twelve barrels making a total of 13,200 fish. Later still they were measured in the *cran*, a willow basket containing 12–1500 fish.

By the early twentieth century, Great Yarmouth was the world's most important herring port. A Fish Wharf was built in 1955 and the 150 boats registered at Yarmouth that year landed six million herring. The previous year twice that had been landed and this marked the beginning of the decline of the fishery.

Curing the herring

The curing of herring was first invented by a Dutchman called William Beukels. The fish were first *gibbed*, which was the removal of the gills and gut, leaving the liver and pancreas in place as that was necessary for the flavour. They were then sprinkled with salt and packed in barrels. With the fish thus preserved, the fleets were able to stay at sea for long periods.

The *Yarmouth bloater* (from the Swedish word *blots* meaning to soak) was invented in 1836 by a local curer called Bishop. The fish was steeped, ungutted, in brine for seven days and then mildly smoked for 6–8 hours, the heat being more important than the smoking. The main season for bloaters was August when the fish were less fatty, having just arrived at the fishing grounds.

Buckling were also left ungutted, but the heads were removed and they were smoked for longer, which made them last longer than the bloaters. Both the bloaters and the buckling were mainly for local consumption, as they did not keep for very long.

Red herring were brined and then smoked for a week which made them much drier. The long-lasting nature of the red herring made it an important staple food in the Middle Ages. Frances Woods, until recently Curator of Chinese History at the British Library, told me an anecdote of how the

The fish finger was invented in 1950 at the Bird's Eye factory in Yarmouth

122

Mongolian invasion of China was temporarily held up by the lack of supply of Yarmouth red herring which fed the army.

Kippers were invented in 1845 by a Newcastle curer, who adapted the Scottish method of curing salmon to the herring. They were gutted, brined and split before smoking. Smoking was done in the smokehouses. After soaking in brine, the fish were washed and then threaded onto wooden *speets*, 21 at a time, by a person called a *riever*. The fish were threaded by inserting the speet into the mouth to emerge at the gills. Men then stacked the smokehouse by laying each speet across the beams of the structure. The smoke was made by lighting hardwood shavings covered with oak sawdust.

Millions of smoked fish were sent abroad each year, mostly to Florence, Venice and Naples, but also to Russia, Poland and Germany, and by 1850 there were sixty curing houses in the town.

The strong smell of the red herring was sometimes used by criminals on the run as it put the hounds off their scent, hence its colloquial use now

Fishermen's Hospital

THE FISHERMEN'S HOSPITAL (above) was built in 1704. Just off the Market Place near St Nicholas Church, it remains a home for the elderly people of the town.

THE NAVAL HOSPITAL was built as a hospital for sailors wounded during the Napoleonic Wars. It was completed in 1811 just before the Wars ended and became, in turn, a barracks, an army mental institution, an army

convalescent home, a navy mental institution, an NHS psychiatric hospital and finally was converted into apartments in 1993.

There remain in Yarmouth some very fine houses along the South Quay (above), two of which have become museums: the Elizabethan House and the Nelson Museum. The wide pavement along the South Quay commands a good view over the river to Southtown.

The Southtown side of the river is on the 'mainland' to the west. The main town of Yarmouth is on the spit of land with the sea behind you as you look across the river.

JOHN SELL COTMAN came to Yarmouth in 1812 at the request of his patron Dawson Turner, who lived at Bank House on the South Quay. Cotman taught Turner's daughter painting while living himself in Southtown, the other side of the river. He returned to Norwich in 1823.

Daniel Defoe travelled through Yarmouth in 1724 and was impressed by the magnificence of the buildings along the South Quay

CHURCHES

Herbert de Losinga, the first Bishop of Norwich, built the Church of St Nicholas, the patron saint of sailors, dedicated in 1119. He also built a Benedictine priory of which little remains now, but parts of the walls can be seen near the church.

He also built Norwich Cathedral and St Margaret's Church, now a Minster, in King's Lynn.

St Nicholas Church, now also a minster, claims to be the largest parish church in the country.

St George's Church is now a theatre. The building on the far right appears to be only one room deep and has a classical façade

FRIARIES

There were three settlements of friars in the town, who preached and cared for the poor. The Whitefriars were Carmelites, the Greyfriars were Franciscan and the Blackfriars were Dominicans. The Augustinian friars had their main friary at Gorleston but had a cell in Yarmouth.

> *A minster church was traditionally one which had its origins in the monastic tradition. It is now a title bestowed by the Church of England on a particularly large or important church.*

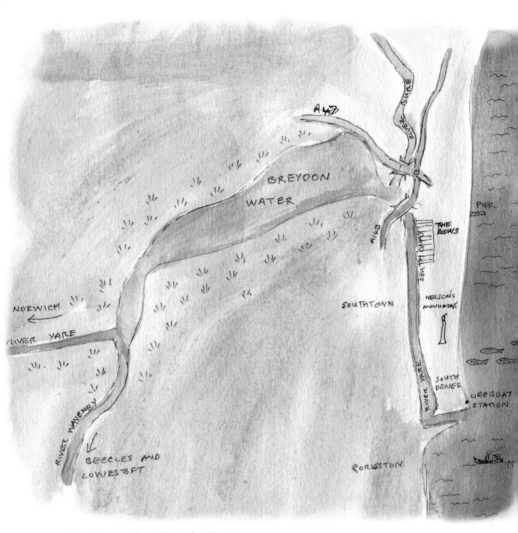

Great Yarmouth and Breydon Water

THE FISHERY IN THE NINETEENTH AND TWENTIETH CENTURIES

From the mid-nineteenth century, with the development of free trade, independent ownership of fishing boats and the coming of the railways, the fishing trade rapidly expanded. Sail began to give way to steam, and then to the petrol and diesel engine, although fishing vessels often still retain a small *staysail* at the stern which helps to give directional stability.

The most successful year ever for the fishery was 1913 when there were 227 Yarmouth registered drifters, and 742 Scottish boats were fishing from Yarmouth. Ninety percent of their catch was exported to Russia.

The Scots

The greatest influence on the development of the Great Yarmouth fishery, after the Dutch, was the increasing involvement of the Scots, who began coming to the town. By 1907, it was estimated that visiting Scots workers, including fishermen, coopers, fisher-girls and curers, swelled the town's population by ten thousand each autumn.

The Scots fisher-girls came with the fleets down the east coast to gut the herring. They worked up to fifteen hours a day gutting thirty fish a minute. They were paid a weekly sum which covered their board and lodging, and then they were given a lump payment at the end of the season. They were known for their extraordinary cheerfulness, despite the working conditions and the state that their hands got into, and for knitting when they were not gutting fish. Most importantly, the Scots developed the markets for pickled herring, and the export of brine-cured herring to Germany and Russia gradually overtook the traditional smoked herring trade. You can see video footage of them working in the Time and Tide Museum.

It was often a family affair, with whole families of south-east coast Scots coming south for the season, the menfolk fishing and their wives and daughters gutting and packing.

Other methods of fishing

Drifting was the best method for catching surface-feeding shoal fish such as the herring. It was usually done at night when the fish would come to the surface to feed and the mesh could not be seen so easily. But around the country, according to the type of fish and the nature of the coast, other methods were adopted.

Long-lining was used in areas where the shores were too rocky for nets which would snag and get damaged. Deep-sea boats would shoot up to four miles of baited line while smaller boats would be happy with a few hundred yards. The great Grand Banks Schooners caught cod like this off the coast of Newfoundland, using small dories which they carried on board. The men would sit in these small open boats all day handling the lines in freezing conditions.

Trawling spread with the development of more powerful sailing boats such as the Brixham Trawler and then the petrol and diesel engines. It became possible to drag heavy trawl nets along the seabed, and fishing began to become much more industrialised, leading as we know now to untold damage to the flora and fauna of the seabed.

The World Wars

During both World Wars many local fishing vessels were requisitioned by the Royal Navy for military service.

Fishermen found themselves at the front line of defence and were employed in many different roles, including balloon barrage, harbour service, hospital ships, torpedo recovery, flare drifting and anti-submarine activities.

In the Second World War, drifters and trawlers were used for mine-sweeping to keep the east coast convoy routes clear for merchant shipping.

The Wars had a dramatic effect on the local economy, with the restriction of fishing and the collapse of the markets to Germany and Russia in the post-war depression.

The first Zeppelin raid in Britain was on Yarmouth in January 1915

The end of the fishery

By the 1920s the scale of the catches began to decline and by 1950 it was clear that centuries of overfishing had decimated the herring stocks.

In 1970 there were just five boats left still fishing, all of them Scottish, and in 1977 herring fishing on the east coast was banned for four years.

The port is now mainly associated with the North Sea oil industry, servicing the oil rigs.

HORATIO NELSON (1758–1805)

Nelson was born in Burnham Thorpe in 1758, joining the Royal Navy as a midshipman and rising to become one of Britain's most distinguished admirals.

He sailed from Yarmouth on many occasions and often stayed at the Star Hotel on South Quay. The original Star Hotel was demolished, the owners relocating it to the adjacent building where it can be found now. The elaborately carved oak panelling which lined the room where Nelson usually stayed was sold to the USA and is now in the Metropolitan Museum in New York.

Nelson was made a Freeman of the town after the Battle of the Nile and this honour was presented to him in The Wrestlers public house in the Market Place, where you can still buy a drink and a bite to eat.

His last battle was the Battle of Trafalgar at which he was fatally wounded by a French sniper. His famous signal to the fleet before the battle was initially meant to read 'England confides that every man will do his duty' but the signaller pointed out that as there was not a specific signal flag for 'confides' it would take a long time to spell out, and suggested substituting 'expects', which did have a dedicated flag. Nelson agreed to this change, and led the fleet to victory.

Nelson was born in Burnham Thorpe and is buried in St Paul's Cathedral

A column was erected in his honour bearing the figure of Britannia looking out to sea. This underwent restoration in 1982 and again in 2004, with the badly eroded stone figure being replaced with a fibreglass replica.

>━● Alexander Scott, Nelson's chaplain on the *Victory*, said about him: *'Let the country mourn their hero; I grieve for the loss of the most fascinating companion I have ever conversed with – the greatest and most simple of men – one of the nicest and most innocent – interesting beyond all, on shore, in public and even in private life. Men are not always themselves and put on their behaviour with their clothes, but if you live with a man on board a ship for years; if you are continually with him in his cabin, your mind will soon find out how to appreciate him. I could forever tell you the qualities of this man. I have not shed a tear for years before 21st October and since, whenever alone, I am quite like a child.'*

CAPTAIN GEORGE MANBY (1765–1854)

In 1807 George Manby, who was the barrack master at the time, witnessed the wrecking of the gun-brig *Snipe* during a gale, only 50 yards off the beach. Sixty-seven men were drowned in full view of the helpless onlookers on the shore. This tragedy inspired him to develop the idea of firing a rope attached to a piece of shot from the shore onto the stricken ship. Known as the Manby Lifesaving Apparatus, it went on to be installed at fifty-nine stations around the coast, saving over a thousand lives.

The rope had to be carefully laid to prevent it tangling and breaking when fired from the rocket

SHOT ROPE

SHALLOW BASKET WITH FAKES OF ROPE

Manby went on to design some of the lifeboats of his time, and he died aged ninety, in Southtown.

THE *LYDIA EVA*

The *Lydia Eva* is the last of the Yarmouth steam drifters and lies for part of the summer on the South Quay at Yarmouth and partly at Lowestoft. She was built in King's Lynn in 1930 for Harry Eastick, who owned several fishing boats in Yarmouth, but the fishing was already in decline and she was sold on only eight years later.

The Air Ministry used her for servicing buoys on the west coast and in 1942 the War Ministry requisitioned her for salvage work. She was subsequently used by the Royal Navy for three years before being acquired by the Maritime Trust as the last example of a steam drifter still afloat. She was a familiar sight in St Katherine's Dock by Tower Bridge in London, until financial problems led to her being laid up at the West India Dock.

The Lydia Eva Charitable Trust was formed with the aim to restore her and bring her back to Yarmouth. This was finally achieved in 1990 and she is now open to the public as a museum.

Sketch of *Lydia Eva*, the last of the steam drifters

FURTHER READING

One of the pleasures of researching this book has been to read the books that others have written about the history of this coast, and to visit the museums and public libraries.

The Time and Tide Museum in Great Yarmouth is a particular favourite. Cromer Museum, the Lifeboat Museums in Cromer and Sheringham, and both True's Yard Fisherfolk Museum and the town museum in King's Lynn are all very rewarding to visit.

The painstaking work of local historians sifting through records has produced a wealth of information and I am grateful to them all for making this information so accessible.

Here are some of the books that I found particularly useful.

Church Ships by Basil Harley
The Edge of the World by Michael Pye
Eel by Richard Schweid
Eighteenth Century Ship-building in Wells by Mike Stammers
Germany, Memories of a Nation by Neil McGregor
The Glaven Ports by Jonathan Hooton
Great Yarmouth by Frank Meeres
Herring: A History of the Silver Darlings by Mike Smylie
King's Lynn by Paul Richards
Medieval Graffiti by Matthew Champion
The Rescues of Henry Blogg by Mick Bensley
Wells: A Small Port and a Wide World by Roger Arguille
The German Ocean by Bryan Ayers
The Ship in the Medieval Economy by Richard Unger
The Pierhead Painters by Roger Finch
The Development of the Rudder by Lawrence V. Mott
Homer's Odyssey, translation by E. V. Rieu
Once Upon a Tide by Godfrey Sayers

For more information about William Faden's map (pp. 70–71),
please see http://www.fadensmapofnorfolk.co.uk/

ACKNOWLEDGEMENTS
Thanks to Godfrey Sayers for allowing me to use his painted copy of the
1586 map of Blakeney Haven (pp. 74–75), and for permitting me to copy
his map of the Blakeney Marshes (pp. 86–87).
Thanks to Cromer Museum for the use of their photograph of Henry Blogg
(p. 96).

I would also like to thank Criss Sandom and Alan Fry for their patience
in coaching me through the finer points of computing.
Celia Ward for help and advice on the practicalities of producing a book.
Bryan Ayers for checking and clarifying the historical details and for providing
me with useful references.
Paul Davies for checking the content relating to Great Yarmouth.
Any remaining errors are entirely mine.